COME ALONG AND SEE

To James
Thanks, Dan

COME ALONG AND SEE

What Some Young Men Did in '48, '49, '50, '51, '52

DAN RASMUSSEN JR.

Copyright © 2014 by Dan Rasmussen Jr.

ISBN: Softcover   978-1-4931-7941-1
        eBook   978-1-4931-7942-8

All rights reserved. No part of this book may be reproduced or transmitted in any form or by any means, electronic or mechanical, including photocopying, recording, or by any information storage and retrieval system, without permission in writing from the copyright owner.

This book was printed in the United States of America.

Rev. date: 10/30/2014

To order additional copies of this book, contact:
Xlibris
1-888-795-4274
www.Xlibris.com
Orders@Xlibris.com
543260

CONTENTS

Nebraska Was Home 9
Getting Acquainted In California 23
Being A Teenager 33
Drafted 49
San Francisco To Yokohama 67
Yokohama To Fox Company 73
Patrol After Patrol And Two Outposts 85
Hill 717, Our Last Outpost 103
Reserve For Awhile And Back Up On The Line 115
Christmas 1951 127
Back To The Line 131
R&R (Rest And Recuperation) 139
Battlefield Promotion 149
Mountains Got Higher 157
First Leg Home 169
Second Leg Home 175
Last Leg Home 179
Epilogue 187

DEDICATION

No two minds think alike. Several people can witness an incident and all describe it differently. This nonfiction story is as I remember it. Some of the things are like they happened yesterday and some are not! I dedicate this book to:

The city of Grand Island, Nebraska, and the city of Long Beach, California—two great towns.

All the guys who spent the first bitter year in Korea (June '50 to June '51).

My friend Glenn Hawkins of Richland, Washington, who sat in his half-track vehicle on the banks of the Yalu River in 1950 and looked across into Manchuria. (President Truman was right in firing MacArthur.) Glenn was awarded three Bronze Stars and wouldn't talk about it. He died of cancer 29 October 1999.

Jim Bowie, who got his shoulder shot up in Korea in 1951. He lives in a veteran's house in Greenwich, Ohio. His wound obviously kept him from living a fulfilled life. Jim has been my pen pal.

Dick Cosh of Grand Island, Nebraska was a classmate of my younger brother and went to Korea right after I got home. I went up to Dick's parents' home and read the first three letters from Dick after he had arrived in Korea. Dick was in the army artillery and I told his parents that that was a good safe place to be. I didn't realize he was a forward observer. He was killed shortly after he got there.

NEBRASKA WAS HOME

A tornado had touched down just west of Cozad, Nebraska. It had made kindling out of six big green billboards that sat along Highway 30. Highway 30 was the main two-lane highway running across the middle of the United States from coast to coast. I was working for the outdoor sign company that owned the billboards that blew down.

It was May 1948. I had graduated from Grand Island Senior High School in January. January sounds like an odd time of the year to be graduating from high school, but it was so. In January of 1935, my kindergarten class was the last of what was called the "mid-termers." The Grand Island school district had a policy of starting school twice a year, once in September and again in January. It wasn't a good policy, so it was being terminated. In evidence, there were only about twelve of us left in our graduating class of 1948, which was too small to hold a graduation ceremony. We could have our diploma, but had to wait until the class behind us graduated in June to take part in ceremony.

Anyway, working for the sign company was my first job in the adult world. I was making thirty-five cents an hour. Normally, I was a billposter's helper, but this week the owner wanted me to go with a construction crew out west to Cozad and help clean up the mess the tornado had made. I was going to go with a foreman, Frank, and his regular helper, Ben. The company owner had just bought his first post-World War II company vehicle. It was a brand new 1947 Dodge stake truck and it was a screaming fire engine red. It was just a truck, with dual wheels in back and a compound low gear and stuff that trucks have, but it was a thing of beauty.

It was only the second year after World War II had ended that new cars and trucks were being made and showing up in town and on the roads. Compared to prewar stuff and army trucks these new vehicles were something to behold. Anyway, this Dodge was Frank's new truck and we were going to Cozad in it.

Monday morning we didn't load anything on the new truck but tools, as we would be loaded down with the old billboards coming home. Cozad was about one hundred miles west of Grand Island and traveling about forty-five miles an hour it was approaching noon when we got there. After checking into the only hotel in town and eating the lunch we had brought, we headed out to survey the mess and determine which end to start at. We didn't get much work done with the remaining few hours of the day.

We ate at the only big restaurant in town that night and every day the rest of the week. There was this cute young waitress working evenings in the restaurant. She kept smiling and making eye contact with me and there was some small talk between the two of us. She was practically asking me if I wanted to take her out. Since the girls weren't exactly falling all over me in high school, it was kind of special that this girl was paying attention to me. Why is it that as you are growing up, a special girl or a neat boy happens along at the wrong time? Not that she was the right girl. There I was, no car, no money, no clothes, and one hundred miles from home. I wasn't in Cozad to start a romance. If there are things that you think you should do with your life, and you're not happy with the stage of your life you are in, it is so hard to walk away from someone you've met that seems to be very special. This cute girl and I never got to that point, as we never went out. But, you do remember, all of your life, the different romances you've had, and maybe the missed opportunities.

Tuesday we put in a hard ten-hour day. The boss wanted all the nails pulled out of the timber and the twisted panels and the severed 4x6's dug out of the ground. We were pooped when we hit the hotel after supper. We had a huge room with three beds in it. The toilet was down the hall.

That night as we were getting ready for bed, Frank all of a sudden said, "You guys want to see my testicle?" Ben and I looked at each other, and then back at Frank. Frank was holding this big bag of lumps and worms in his hands and saying, "Isn't this something?" It sure was. Ben and I looked at it as he moved the lumps and worms around in his hands. When he let go of it, his scrotum hung halfway to his knees and was ugly and it looked like it had to hurt and you felt sorry for him.

Ben evidently hadn't seen it before and asked Frank, "Gee, what caused that to happen?"

Frank answered back, "I don't know. It started years ago and just keeps getting bigger." As he lifted it up again and was looking at it he said, "The darn thing is heavy and uncomfortable. Maybe there is a whole pint of blood stored in the darn thing." In 1948 if you were poor, you didn't go to a doctor unless you were dying. A lot of us were poor and that's the way it was. You didn't see a dentist either. You just let your teeth rot out and then got false teeth. So, that was the way it was with Frank. He was just living with his affliction.

We only worked eight hours Wednesday and Thursday as Frank could tell we would have it all cleaned up and the truck loaded with half of the busted stuff by Thursday night. Friday morning we went across Highway 30 from the demolished billboards and laid out the holes for a new billboard. Frank had been given the information for locating this sign. Ben and I were digging the holes for the uprights and anchors with posthole diggers. Frank was watching me and finally said to me, "You don't go around and around that hole like you're circling covered wagons. You plant your feet across the hole and you don't move 'em until you're finished with the hole." He wasn't being mean about it. It was all in fun. It does work, especially if the soil is rock free. It reminded me of the time when I was working at the supermarket when I was about fourteen. I was sweeping the aisle with a bristle broom and flipping lettuce leaves and stuff six feet down the aisle when the manager came up to me and said, "You're raising too much dust and commotion. You're supposed to stand to the side and pull that stuff like this." And then he gave me a demonstration. Boy, the stuff you have to learn when you are growing up!

Friday afternoon we drove the now-used truck back to Grand Island. The next week I went back to my regular job of putting the posters on the billboards.

There were twelve to fifteen separate sheets of paper that made up these posters. We would put them up using long handled brushes. Working from the ground, it was tricky to lay a folded sheet across your brush and slowly coax it up the face of the billboard and make it stick to a pre-pasted area. Then you would carefully unfold it with your brush making the whole sheet stick on the paste. If you got it positioned close to where it was supposed to be, you were doing great. You could slide the whole sheet a little on the paste, but not too far! Doing this two to six feet over your head and in the wind was a challenge. We would travel around central Nebraska and put up new posters over the old ones once a month. We even had some billboards down along the Kansas border around Red Cloud and Superior, Nebraska. These large billboards were a very popular form of advertising across the entire United States. Of course, there were lots of Coca Cola posters and other popular products, but the favorite of us guys was the Sealy mattress ones. They usually had a female model in a nighty, comfortably posed on the mattress.

It was the first part of July. I came home on a Friday night from work and my parents told me my sister Maxine had called and said there was a billposter's job for me in Long Beach, California! My parents could see the disbelief and concern on my face since my eyes and mouth were wide open. We immediately began to talk about the things I would have to do to get ready. I had to jump at the opportunity. Nebraska wasn't too good a place for young people to find work in. Other states like California often lured good talent out of Nebraska with offers of better paying jobs. I didn't like going up to my boss's house and telling him I had to quit to go to California to post billboards. He said it was OK and that he would send a letter of recommendation, which I never got.

Monday morning I boarded the *City of Los Angeles* streamliner at the Grand Island Depot. I was leaving home, leaving my brother Jack, my parents, and the only house I had ever lived in, leaving the memories. My brother Jack was a year and a half younger than I was. He and I were still sleeping together which we had done for about sixteen years. It was we two in a crib in the beginning. Later we began sleeping upstairs in that bedroom that was freezing cold in the wintertime and unbearably hot in the summertime. Upstairs where the cold north wind would blow the wailing whistles of the freight trains right against the single pane of our window. The main east-west Union Pacific rail lines passed through Grand Island. They followed Highway 30 much of the way. There was an endless stream of freight and passenger trains during the war years of 1939 to 1946. Hauling men and equipment across our country at a frantic pace made it easy to tell it was a serious period of time in our country. A lot of freight trains had one hundred cars between the engine and the caboose. We would meet relatives from Dannebrog, Nebraska, which was twenty-four miles away, and picnic at a park along the Union Pacific tracks. Counting those one hundred freight cars that included tankers, flat cars, and boxcars was fun. Today, they can put 150 cars on a freight train because they have made the curves and bends straighter. West of Cheyenne, Wyoming, there was a steep grade called Sherman Hill. The freights going west had to pull it, and it was so steep and long that it would make any steam engine whine and wail. They would often add another engine at Cheyenne to help pull the heavy freights up Sherman Hill. The extra engine was then disconnected and the lone engine was on its own to get across the rest of the Rocky Mountains.

Grand Island had an army air base during World War II. It was a stopover preparation and training base for bombers like the B-17. All kinds of stuff was checked and added to the aircraft at the base. These giant four-engine planes had been built at Boeing Aircraft Company in the Seattle,

Washington area. They were on their way to England to join the U.S. and English Air Force and their heroic efforts to slow down Hitler and his world-conquering ideas. The B-29 was processed through in the later years of the war and sent mainly to the Pacific theater.

My dad was a painter by trade and got some good steady higher paying work at the air base while it was being prepared and maintained. With that money, Mom and Dad could afford to have natural gas brought into the house and we got a stand-alone heater put in the living room and one in the kitchen. Mom got rid of the old wood and coal cooking stove too, and got a nice gas range. Just after the war, I helped dad dig the trench for the soil pipe to a septic tank and we got an indoor bathroom put in. Here's one for you. In 1833, the first indoor bathroom was installed in the White House in Washington D.C. It included a tub, sink, and a water closet (toilet). In 1943, 110 years later, some of the masses were catching up.

There were a lot of army personnel at the Grand Island Air Base during the war years. Many people in Grand Island made their basements into apartments to house these extra people and made some extra money that way. My brother and I were caddies in '42 and '43 at our Riverside nine-hole golf course. There was an air force captain, whose last name was Fish, that my brother and I caddied for many times. We have never forgotten him. Funny eh? He was a handsome physical specimen that seemed to be a natural leader. He would always strip to the waist, shoot par golf, and pay us a dollar for eighteen holes. The going rate was seventy-five cents. He was kind of an all-business individual, but an example and inspiration to a couple of young kids. With so many flyboys in town, and many of the other men gone to war, the young airmen had lots of women to date and take out. About nightfall, a couple of times, us boys got up on the swimming pool bathhouse roof and waited for couples to come to Pier Park. Then we would watch them roll around in the grass and make out. Grand Island also had an ordnance plant outside of town that made bombs and smaller projectiles like bazooka and mortar rounds. People that worked in the powder rooms would turn yellow. Their hands, faces, and hair would turn yellowish. It was funny to see them running around town.

The stock market started its crash and the Great Depression set in the year I was born, 1929. Mom and Dad nursed us six kids through the Depression with secondhand clothes, a big garden, and chickens in the chicken yard. My four sisters found housework and waitressing jobs and had to give some of the money they made to Mom and Dad. My four pretty sisters were ten to fourteen years older than my brother and I. I know they changed our diapers and gave us baths many times. Gee, how embarrassing. But when you think of how nice and pretty they were, maybe it wasn't such a bad deal after all. Mildred married young and went to Wisconsin with her new husband. During 1940, Elaine, Maxine, and Dorothy all went to Southern California. Mom and Dad had two stars in the window during World War II for having two children in the service. Maxine had joined the WAVES and Elaine had joined the WACS.

And now Maxine was calling and saying, "Hurry out here. They need a billposter at Foster and Kleiser and they are holding the job open for you." Maxine's father-in-law worked for Foster and Kleiser as a mechanic. He took care of the fleet of cars, heavy trucks, and panel trucks that the company had. He knew they were short of a billposter and casually mentioned me to Brooks, the billposting manager.

"Sure," Brooks said, "get him out here and we'll give him the job."

So, as the prestigious *City of Los Angeles* was leaving Grand Island behind, I thought about a few other things. My 1932 four-door Chevrolet was my most precious possession, such as it was. (The mechanical brakes were oh so bad.) I bought it in 1946, as I was turning sixteen, with the $200 I had been saving for six years. Boy, for $200 there wasn't much to choose from on the used car lots. The whole country had wrung the last mile out of the cars made in the 1930s. The engine was shot in my Chevy. It had a cracked block and burned oil. But, you know, that six-cylinder engine would start on cold Nebraska mornings. It had a good reputation for doing that. I drove it to school for two years, sometimes running on five cylinders. I also drove it to Kearney, Nebraska one Friday night to watch our great basketball team play the Kearney High School team. My buddy, Laverne Weinman, went with me. That was a tough ninety-mile round trip for my old car.

Grand Island was state basketball champ in both '47 and '48. We had some great athletes those two years. Bob Reynolds was one of them. He was a starter on both the '47 and '48 teams. He went on to play football for the University of Nebraska and became known as Mr. Touchdown USA. My buddy Laverne had a '33 Ford sedan with a V-8 engine in it. It would perform circles around my '32 Chevy. We took Laverne's Ford to Lincoln, Nebraska to the '47 state basketball championship. That was an easy 180-mile round trip for his car, but just outside Lincoln on the way home his headlights went out. We spent much of the night getting home. If a car was coming we had to get off the road. Otherwise, we drove ten to fifteen miles per hour as we both hung our heads out the window trying to follow a dark centerline and the side of the road. More fun.

Now that I was leaving, I told my dad and brother to sell my car as soon as they could since I would need the money to get some kind of car in California. I loved working on my old car. I took welding in high school and in the school shop it was pretty exciting when I braised a split fender on my Chevy with brass welding rod. Grand Island had a great school system. They gave us a good education from kindergarten through twelfth grade. One day in grade school, my pencil needed sharpening. This was in the fourth grade at Wasmer Grade School. Miss Selk was our teacher. It was the winter of 1939 and I was nine years old. The sharpener was over by the window. When I got over there and looked out, there was my dad across the street going door to door asking people if he could shovel the snow from their sidewalk. He had a scoop shovel over his shoulder. We'd had a five-inch snowfall the night before. Two feelings flooded my mind! I was so sorry my dad didn't have a steady job and I didn't want my classmates to know that my dad was across the street trying to make fifty cents shoveling snow. This equaled peer pressure deluxe on a young fellow. I wasn't mature enough to realize lots of dads didn't have steady jobs.

The Depression still gripped many families and would for a couple more years. More than one jobless man got a peanut butter sandwich on homemade bread from my mom for sharpening a knife or her scissors. They were hungry and would barter for a sandwich. My dad could have given them a glass of beer. He made the best homebrewed beer. Us kids would get a sip now and then or drink the sediment at the bottom of the bottle. With no money for entertainment, a glass of beer after a hard day's work made life a little more bearable. When you had work, the workweek was six days long. You got Sunday off. The majority of families were making their own beer during Prohibition, which was federal law from 1920 to 1933. Prohibition made it illegal to make or sell alcoholic beverages with more than 0.5 percent alcohol. This law turned the taverns into speakeasies, the gangsters into bootleggers, and the Mafia came on big time. It didn't cost too much to make a batch of beer. My mom and dad had a ten-gallon crock to make the beer in. It sat in the kitchen while the water, malted barley, and yeast went to work converting fermentable sugars into alcohol. They had enough quart bottles to handle the batch. Bottling night was a big event. With a siphon hose, a box of bottle caps, and the hand-operated bottle capper, it didn't take too long to fill thirty-five to forty bottles. Then down into the cool cellar they went. In the weeks after, every once in awhile in the dark cool cellar, a bottle would blow its cap off with a bang. We would all look at each other and grin.

Thinking more about school, my sister Mildred set a girls' high jump record at Barr Jr. High School in 1933. That record held until thirteen years later, when Frankie Page in my brother's class bested it. Being barely above average in sports, I had a great feeling of pride and accomplishment when I lettered in track at Barr Junior High. I pole-vaulted and ran the relay with four other guys. I got to buy and wear the orange school sweater with a purple and a white stripe. We were sure lucky to have a small athletic program in the middle of World War II. We competed against the other junior high school in town.

In senior high woodworking class, I made a pair of wall pin-up lamps. They were pretty popular lighting fixtures in the '40s and '50s. Using white holly and walnut wood, I cut sixteen pieces that went into the two lamps and bored the holes for the electrical cord and light socket and glued them together. They went together nice and were looking good. The last step was a coat of varnish. That night as they were drying in the paint room someone stole them. For the next two days, Mr. Keister, the shop teacher, was pretty upset. Each of his classes got the same speech. "Last night, as you have probably heard, we had a pair of pin-up lamps stolen out of the paint room." He continued, "I think stealing from your classmates is a pretty low thing to do. Or, if it was an outsider, I want to know that too. I'm offering a five dollar reward for information leading to the return of the lamps." No one came forth with any information. I had two moral rewards from this thievery. Someone thought my work was nice enough to steal and Mr. Keister exempted me from the final exam, the only one in the class. About four months after our graduation, one of my friends told me where my lamps were. He said, "They're out on the farm, up on the wall, in this guy's bedroom." And it was a classmate. We know who you are!

Poor Carl Dittman. He was a classmate who was taking auto mechanics in our high school. He was going through the engine of his '33 Chevy in the class shop. He removed the head and gave it a valve job, put in new rings, and tightened the main and the connecting rod bearings. He had it all back together and was going to put the spark plugs in the next day and fire it up. Sometime after school or that night, someone dropped a nut that would fit a quarter twenty bolt into one of the spark plug holes. When Carl put the plugs in the next day and started the engine, the nut was driven down through the top of the piston and into the crankcase in a sickening sound of stressed metals. Carl had to tear the whole engine down again and put in a new piston. Even in 1947 we had little envious bully monsters in amongst us!

Growing up, in spite of the Depression and World War II, was great fun. The candy Easter egg hunts in Pioneer Park, before the black birds took over the American elm trees, were exciting to us little kids. So were the season tickets to the first class swimming pool that the city built in about 1936. Our hair would turn green from the chlorine. We would spend a week during the summer on the Platt River with the Boy Scouts. Mr. Schafer was a great scoutmaster. His son's name was Laverne and was a starter on that '47 state championship basketball team. Grand Island was a great place to grow up.

The streamliner was somewhere in Wyoming now, and it was suppertime. I wandered back through several cars to the dining car. It was pretty elegant looking and it made me a little nervous. They had tablecloths, sterling silver dinnerware, crystal glassware, and fresh flowers at each table. It was not exactly what I was used to. After eating I left a ten percent tip. The black waiter looked at it and told me, "That tip is not enough, sir. I cannot accept that," and walked off with his nose in the air. Somewhat belittled and rattled, my brain finally knew what half of 10% was, and I added that and got out of there.

You had to spend one night on the train going from Grand Island to Los Angeles. When you traveled coach, like I was, you had to sleep sitting up.

GETTING ACQUAINTED IN CALIFORNIA

Tuesday morning, the streamliner pulled into the Los Angeles railroad depot. I had to catch a bus that went to Long Beach. Maxine was waiting for me when I arrived at the Long Beach bus terminal. We caught a local bus home to her and husband Bob's apartment. Thursday morning Bob took me to the Foster and Kleiser Company and introduced me to Brooks, the manager of the billposting section. Bob knew some of these guys through his dad, who had thrown my name into the hat, and also because Bob worked at an auto body repair shop next door, where Foster and Kleiser would get bodywork done. There was a little chitchat and then Bob went off to his job. I know the manager was a little surprised to see this skinny eighteen-year-old kid who didn't need to shave every day standing in front of him. I weighed 135 pounds and hadn't reached my six feet of height. He was nice though. There wasn't any problem.

He had me sign some stuff and told me it was a union job and that I would be making $1.25 an hour. He suggested I buy a pair of striped bib overalls, as that was what all the guys wore. "You can stuff the end blanking paper into the bib. Works real good," he told me. "And how about being here tomorrow morning at eight A.M. ready to work?" I said, "Sure, you bet." Then I shook his hand and said, "Thank you."

Four working days had passed and I had gone from making thirty-five cents an hour to $1.25 an hour. That was about three and a half times what I was making back home. To say the least, I was pretty excited about being in California. My sister and I got to the store and bought me two pair of striped overalls and a lunch bucket.

The Foster and Kleiser shops were only five blocks from my sister's apartment, so it was an easy walk to my first day of work. But, wouldn't you know, as often happens to the new man, they put me with the worst S.O.B. in the billposting department. I didn't know this at first. We loaded our paste and water tanks and blanking paper and packed in a day's supply of posters and headed for San Pedro. On the way he didn't say a word and I was getting the feeling he was unhappy about something. I also noticed there wasn't a crank handle on my window, like it was deliberately missing. When we got to our first billboard he mumbled, "I'll show you how to hang the scaffold." We had a scaffold hanging on the side of the panel truck. It had a center ladder with a hook, two metal end rods with hooks, and two wooden planks that were supported by the ladder and end rods.

We didn't use scaffolds in Nebraska, so this was all new to me. After we had hung the scaffold, he gave me a smoothing brush and holster that was to be belted around my waist. He filled two buckets with paste and a third bucket with water. He took a paste bucket and the poster we were supposed to put on the billboard, and headed for the billboard. I knew I was supposed to bring my paste bucket and the water bucket. By the time I got headed for the billboard he was already up the ladder and out on his plank. I didn't see how he had gone up the ladder and got out on his plank. Well, the bottom rung of the ladder was almost four feet off the ground and I couldn't see how in the world I was going to get my two buckets up there when you'd be doing good to get yourself up on that bottom rung. I really thought he would come halfway down the ladder and I would hand the buckets up to him. Well, he wasn't coming halfway down, so I said to him. "How do you get these buckets up there?" He exclaimed rather loud, "For Jesus Christ," and bolted down the ladder and grabbed both of my buckets by the sides of the handles, hoisted them up and grabbed the sides of the ladder, did the four-foot splits and up the ladder he went. I kind of thought, "Jesus Christ," to myself as I went up the ladder empty-handed. I usually only have to be shown things one time unless they're complicated. I knew how to paste and put the poster on and I knew when something was straight and this helped because he wanted a nice-looking poster when he was finished. We worked steady all day long and put up thirteen posters.

Thirteen posters was a good average day's work for any of the crews. And you know, as onerous as he was, I know he wanted to put up thirteen posters that first day to not only work my ass off, but to also show the managers that I was indeed a billposter and deserved to be kept on. But the tone had been set. His personality was such that he was always disgusted, onerous, particular, unhappy, and no one wanted to work with him. The posters on this guy's route were always brightly bordered and sharp looking. But that missing crank on the window of the helper's side of the truck was enough to make you want to kick him in the teeth. On a hot California afternoon, you had to crawl into that mostly closed-up panel truck and he was the only one that had any air.

Whenever the cranky guy and I were in San Pedro, we would eat the lunch we carried in MacArthur Park, which was part of Fort MacArthur. Fort MacArthur was named after General Douglas MacArthur and was an army installation covering a point of land sticking out to sea. The park overlooked the port of San Pedro full of worldwide shipping and was pretty and impressive. San Pedro had a wino problem. Winos were guys without a job or home, and were addicted to the alcohol in wine. More than one lived behind our billboards in makeshift cardboard shelters. It was kind of sad. I worked about nine months with old cranky and then went on the Long Beach City route with a real nice guy and eventually worked all the regions covered by the Long Beach branch of Foster and Kleiser.

Foster and Kleiser Outdoor Advertising Company was a large company with their main shops in Los Angeles. With their branches in Long Beach and San Diego, they had the coastline of Southern California smothered in advertising. And it wasn't just the big green billboards with the monthly paper posters. They had, I thought, some fine artists that worked with oils and paints producing giant forty—to eighty-foot long semi-permanent signs. These artists would paint in some detail, lavish signs for the larger businesses, especially department stores, but covered it all from food to oil. They might paint beautiful women wearing fashionable clothing for Buffums or Broadway department stores, or paint the huge head of a man smoking a Camel cigarette. This guy, with a mechanical smoke generator behind the billboard, through his pursed lips, would blow a real three foot smoke ring—a real attention getter. It was so interesting to walk through the large studio-like room that these artists had and see what they were up to next. Large signs like these were painted on sections of steel panels that were then separated and put into a nice wood frame out on a highway or a busy boulevard.

The Long Beach Foster and Kleiser shops were located on Magnolia Boulevard. It was a beautiful wide street lined with ornamental magnolia trees. In 1948 this boulevard seemed new, the shop buildings were of Spanish architecture and seemed new, and it seemed like the whole of Southern California was new and virgin and full of romance and glamour. For the next two and a half years I would travel up and down the Pacific Coast Highway from the city of Manhattan Beach, just South of Los Angeles, down to San Juan Capistrano, which was forty miles South of Long Beach. We would drive to and post billboards in all the famous beach towns. There was Hermosa Beach, Redondo Beach, San Pedro, Long Beach, Belmont Shores, Seal Beach, Sunset Beach, Huntington Beach, Newport Beach, Balboa, Corona Del Mar, Laguna Beach, and Capistrano Beach. We had a billboard across the street from the Mission San Juan Capistrano where the famous swallows would return about the same time every year. All these beach towns had miles of bathing beaches along the warm Pacific Ocean. We would also go about thirty miles inland to towns like Downey, Whittier, Fullerton, Anaheim, and Santa Ana.

My, oh my, what an adventure this was for a sheltered kid from Nebraska. And it was an adventure also, to post billboards on rooftops. You had to be cautious leaning out over the sidewalk two stories up! Starting in the fall of each year, after there were about twelve layers of posters on the billboards, the paper would start to crack and come loose from the panels. Then it was scraping season. With brute force and a straight, hoe-like cutting tool we'd clean off all the old stuff down to the steel panels. We were cautious during this procedure too, as billboards have always been a popular target for .22-caliber rifles and other weapons. Where the bullet goes through, the steel is stressed into sharp edges. When you hit these sharp edges with the power stroke of your hoe-like cutting tool, it can stop abruptly, and the momentum of the action can throw you off your plank and down to the concrete or worse. I went off twice. I just jumped off into a plowed field both times. You're not so careful scraping when you have a soft landing below. Guys would get busted up falling off their scaffold for one reason or another. We would hear about it at our union meetings. Scraping season was hard work and meant some overtime.

Long Beach was the prettiest place I had ever seen. Palm trees were everywhere. These palm trees always seemed different from one another. The bottom branches always die each year and slap themselves down on the trunk of the tree. You have the option of cutting these dead hanging fan type branches off of the trunk or letting them just hang there and accumulate year after year. If you let them accumulate, the trunk of your palm tree can grow to resemble a pineapple. If you chop these branches off real close to the trunk, you can keep the trunk real skinny and in time have a neat forty-foot palm tree on stilts. Actually, most cities have an ordinance that requires you to cut the dead fan-like branches off because as they accumulate they make a nice home for rodents and other undesirables.

One of the first things I had to do, since I now lived in California, was to register for the draft. All eighteen-year-olds had to do this. I was already registered in Nebraska, but you had to register again if you moved to another state.

In Long Beach, there was oil, oil everywhere. It seemed like those crazy teeter-totter pumps were everywhere, sucking that black gold out of the pools underground. Oftentimes, there would be one right next to the billboard we were posting. The darn things fascinated me. I often thought though, that if there was a huge pool of oil under where we were working, what if the ground gave way and we fell in! Signal Hill in Long Beach was dotted with teeter-totter pumps. Signal Hill was a good-sized hill that was high enough to afford a spectacular view of Long Beach, the ocean, and on up toward Los Angeles and Hollywood. At night the lights of the cities and the darkened skies were a sight for lovers. And despite the pumping oil wells, it was a popular romantic place to take your girl to park, enjoy each other, and the view.

The oil that was coming out of these wells had an asphalt base as compared to a paraffin base as oil from the eastern U.S. This made it heavier and harder to refine, but it was a good oil and excellent for paving asphalt boulevards and highways. And pave they did. Beautiful wide four-lane boulevards crisscrossed the entire Los Angeles and Long Beach areas and four-lane highways were paved up and down the coast. (Freeways hadn't been invented yet.) This oil was excellent for orange grove smudge pots too. And smudge they did! Coming into Southern California from the East, on a two-lane highway, you would drive through miles and miles of beautiful orange groves. These groves, when they were ten or more miles inland from the ocean, where susceptible to temperatures dropping below freezing in the wintertime. Igniting these smudge pots, full of this California oil, would make a rather putrid layer of hydrocarbons over the trees and save the young buds and fruit from freezing.

I lived with my sister Dorothy and her husband Paul in Bellflower during the winter of 1948. Bellflower was about ten miles inland from Long Beach and in orange grove country. It often froze there in the wintertime. Even with the windows and doors shut tight, on the nights they smudged, we would wake up with soot all around our noses in the morning. That's how serious the operation was and on frost nights this oil smoke could lie all across Los Angeles and was the forerunner to California smog.

I could never put my finger on just what it was that Long Beach air smelled like, but I loved the smell whatever it was. To me the air smelled like a combination of salt sea air and oil. And the smell would change as the afternoon ocean breezes blew in. The smell of the air on a dense foggy night was all ocean smell. It seemed like all those tiny driblets of fog had filtered out all the dirt and stuff in the air, and the air was so clean you wanted to breath in deep and be invigorated. You could kind of feel the driblets of fog fall on your face. Ah, ocean fog—beautiful, mysterious, dangerous, and hypnotizing if you drove in it too long.

Long Beach had a naval station, and sea ports too. It also had fish canneries on Terminal Island. If you got close enough, and the wind was right, you could smell the process.

Standard Oil, Union Oil, and Richfield were some of the big oil companies in operation. My best friend Joe worked for one of them. He was on the operating floor of the cracking plant one night when an explosion engulfed the whole operating gallery. Joe and a half dozen other guys were just able to crawl to the exits on their bellies as flames were licking their backsides and trying to suck every breath out of them.

The broad thoroughfare, Ocean Boulevard in downtown Long Beach, ran along the oceanfront. On the landside of Ocean Boulevard there were several plush 1940s movie theaters. Some 1940s theaters in large cities had unbelievable luxuries. Some had curving staircases on each side of the lobby leading up to the mezzanine where the balcony and fancy restrooms were. There were beautiful chandeliers, statues, and water fountains. The whole place would be carpeted with plush pile. Of course they sold popcorn and candy bars, but there weren't any soft drinks sold to spill all over the place and make everything sticky.

Upper class shopping facilities were on Ocean Boulevard too. One store had a two-story glass corner front. They had put rotating mannequins on each floor and would dress them in furs and fancy gowns and stuff like that. The swanky Riviera Hotel was up the boulevard. This multistoried, round building gave the wealthy tenants a great view inland and out to sea. Also on the ocean side of Ocean Boulevard was the famous Pike amusement park with its Cyclone roller coaster, the Plunge swimming facility, merry-go-rounds, and other rides and countless side attractions. It was a first class, clean, safe, year-round amusement park for young and old, and boy was it popular. Off and on we spent many hours down there. The Cyclone roller coaster was big time Long Beach. Wow, what fun! The Long Beach Auditorium for higher cultured things was next to the Pike.

For a kid from the plains of Nebraska, Long Beach was eye popping and beautiful. I couldn't wait for the next day to begin.

BEING A TEENAGER

My sister Maxine had joined a small Lutheran church on Pine Street in Long Beach and got me to go to church with her and her husband Bob. It was a good thing to be doing for all of us. This small congregation was actually a breakaway from a larger Lutheran church. They broke away because the board members of the big church committed church funds while the pastor was on vacation, making the pastor very angry. He took a third of the congregation with him and started this small church.

The little church was struggling in several areas, one of them being the choir. So, there were several invitations for me to join the choir, which I did. I love to sing and did in school choirs, but reading notes was not one of my strong points. Some Sundays there would only be five or six of us trying to struggle through our song before the sermon. Anyway, at church I met some kids, who knew some more kids, and it wasn't too long before I had some friends to run around with.

A couple of guys named Joe and Henry were fast becoming my friends. Henry was a handsome guy with a square jaw. He was already twenty-one. Joe was good looking too, with a more pointed nose and curly hair.

One Sunday afternoon Joe, Henry, and I stopped in at the house of two sisters we knew from church. These girls were from a wealthy family and lived in a fancy house. Their parents were in the food business and were big contributors to the small church we all went to. They had a round ten-inch TV console in their living room, something only the rich had in 1948. These girls had a girlfriend over that Sunday. She occasionally came to our church too, so we all knew each other. Their parents were not at home.

When someone asked, "What should we do?" Joe jokingly said, "We can play strip poker." The girls squealed and the six of us sat on the den rug and started dealing the cards. This was all in fun and we expected everyone to chicken out in a hurry. As the cards were dealt and the poker hands were made, there was a shoe coming off here and there, but it wasn't too long before I had both shoes and socks off. Someone else would lose a shoe and then it came back to me. I was sitting there naked from the waist up. My shirt was gone and my T-shirt was gone and the girls were squealing and there was much laughter. I only had my pants left and it didn't seem possible the cards could go against me anymore. But again, I had the lowest poker hand. Pandemonium! The one sister hollered over the din, "Go to the upstairs bathroom and put a towel around you."

Being a good sport and with much encouraging laughter, I disappeared up the staircase. I took off my pants, wrapped a bath towel around my shorts, and to loud applause, I made my descent down the stairs. I made a feeble attempt to sit down on the floor to continue play, but could see it was going to be impossible to do with the towel around my bottom. I said, "I guess this is as far as we can go with this. We gotta quit." They all understood as I headed back upstairs to put my clothes on. If their parents had come home and caught me running around their house mostly naked, I may have been in trouble. The youngest sister was only fourteen.

It was with these girls that we went swimming several times at the Long Beach lagoon. The lagoon was a finger of salt water that came inland. The city had put in a mesh screen at the inlet to keep stingrays out, so it was a popular swimming hole. We would play horse and rider with the girls straddling our necks in the water. The girls would pull and tug at each other trying to topple their opponent and her horse. When you put a 130-pound girl on your shoulders and get jerked around in chest deep water, it's fun, but God, it's hard work.

Going to the beaches of the beautiful blue Pacific Ocean was always a treat. Well, most of the time. During those two and a half years I was doing this, there were a couple of things that bothered me. Every other time you went swimming, low and behold, there would be a dead stingray lying in the sand. Now, these guys are ugly. They were usually about fifteen to eighteen inches across, kind of round, with the tapering outer sides of their body acting like wings for propulsion. They had a white underbelly and were gray on top. Now, here is the worst part. These guys had a stinger at the end of a whip-like tail that was about as long as their body. The word was that the venom from their stinger could be fatal if you were stung in the stomach, but if stung in the arm or leg, it was like a rattlesnake bite. It wouldn't do the nervous system or circulatory system any good. I don't know how these stingrays wound up dead on the beach, but I think fishermen probably caught them fishing from the shoreline.

Now, take kelp. Kelp is a slimy bulbous leaf mass that grows in beds along the shores. It would rise and fall with the waves coming in, so it would be on the move all the time. When all of a sudden some kelp would brush up against your leg, your mind would panic, "Could that be a stingray?" I never heard of anyone getting stung. I think you would have to pretty much step on one for it to sting you. Like so many earthly creatures, they are more afraid of you than you of them.

The other thing that worried me about the ocean happened down at Huntington Beach. We had figured out that the best waves for body surfing and fun were at Huntington Beach, so we went there a lot. One day, when us three guys were down there, the waves were weird and we just had the best time and laughed our heads off. Those waves would sustain themselves clear to the sand of the beach. So when you could catch them and ride them with your body, the wave would dump you out on the sand and we would laugh thinking that was the ride of a lifetime. I wonder if something was going on with that ocean that day. Normally ocean waves break over and peter out into a foot or two of water about thirty to forty feet from the shoreline.

It was about midmorning on this day that the three of us arrived at Huntington Beach to go swimming. We parked the car, stripped down to our swimsuits, and headed for the beach. The ocean was unusually calm that morning, but gosh, it could be pretty calm most mornings. It would stay that way until the wind and tide got to pushing bigger and bigger breakers in as the day wore on. But, there were no breakers at all. Not even little bitty guys.

Side by side, we started to wade out into the ocean. It was easy walking and we didn't even realize it. It was like we were kind of hypnotized. Further and further out we walked. As the water went over our shoulders and we were out there up to our necks, we stopped and could immediately feel the sand being washed from under our feet and outgoing water pressure on our lower legs. There was an undertow! We knew we had to carefully get the hell out of there. It seemed our instincts told us that to pop to the surface and start swimming to shore would be a mistake. The water on top was probably going out too, but at a slower rate. All three of us quickly turned around. As the sand was disappearing from under our feet, we had to lean into the outgoing water and take a quick short step toward the beach. In an instant the sand was disappearing again, so another short step was necessary. Instinct again told us that we needed to stay upright and keep our feet anchored to the bottom or be swept out to sea. It was scary. Moving about six inches at a time we finally got our shoulders out of the water and then our chests were out and we were going to be all right. I don't remember any of us saying a single word about anything while this took place. That day, the water on the surface was going out too, so this crazy water may have been more like a riptide. Anyway, it scared all three of us half to death. We did get the hell out of there and were pretty quiet driving back to Long Beach.

Beaches back in those days were never crowded. There was no one else around that morning at Huntington Beach. Us three guys were not native Californians. We were from New York, Illinois, and Nebraska. Killer rip currents can be present in most oceans. They are a deceptively calm swath of water and can be as wide as half a football field. Hawaii has them, but you never hear talk about them. In 1998 there were ten people swept to their deaths around San Francisco by these potent currents. Some of their beaches post warnings about these currents.

Fishing in the ocean was popular for food and fun. My brother-in-law Bob had a couple of old boats. One of these old things had an inboard four-cylinder Willis engine, but the transmission only had a reverse gear. Heading out to sea with the butt end of the boat going first was pretty weird. Of course, we'd have to come back in the same way.

Usually, after getting bait from the bait barge, we would just go outside the breakwater, drop anchor, and fish right there. This is where you could always catch bonito. Bonito is a member of the Mackerel family, but you would think it was a bona fide piranha. This fish, when caught about twelve to fifteen feet deep, could usually be pulled straight up and into the boat. Then watch out. They would run twelve to eighteen inches in length with the front two inches all mouth and many teeth about an eighth of an inch long. They would go wild in the boat, flopping all over the place. When you finally got hold of them, you had to avoid their teeth by using a pair of pliers to get the hook out. As many as we caught, I was never around when they were fried up. To this day I wonder what they tasted like.

Us three boys even rented a rowboat one morning and went fishing for them. The rental guy said, "You don't go outside the breakwater with this rowboat!" We rowed out to the breakwater. The ocean was real calm looking, so we snuck around the end of the breakwater and threw in our lines. In just a few minutes we realized the swells were pretty big and getting bigger, so we got back behind the breakwater where it was safe. We didn't have much luck that morning, but we did catch a ten-inch fish that was so ugly it was scary to have him in the boat with us. He was gray and black with humps and lumps and warts all over him and a row of spiny fins down his back. We were told it was a California scorpion fish and his spiny fins were poisonous. Gee, it isn't safe anywhere.

I had another friend from church whose name was Charlie. He was a very good soloist. He sang in the choir and sang a lot of solos for Sunday services. He heard the grunion were running and was all excited when he told me, "We gotta go get us some grunion." Grunion are a small silvery fish that are food for bigger fish, but people like to eat them too. They run about four inches long and spawn at night on the beaches of the ocean. They'll come in on one wave, lay their eggs in the sand, and go back out on the next several waves. Charlie and I had stopped and got a pint of gin to take with us that night we went grunion hunting. All of us teenage boys started to act like big shots and started drinking beer and liquor and smoking cigarettes. None of us ever got in trouble with it. We both only had a couple small sips from the bottle that night. It was mainly manly symbolism.

Charlie seemed to know where to go and wait for these grunion. We were down at Seal Beach and crossed a No Trespassing barricade into a naval reserve area. We were at water's edge, barefooted with our pant legs rolled up over our knees. We had a quarter moon out, so there was some light. We had brought along a gunnysack. The small waves were lapping the beach. All of a sudden, and this is unbelievable, we were standing in fish up to our ankles. Those fish created so much busy activity, that flying sand was dense three feet off the beach and even higher. A bit shook up because of what was going on, it took us a few seconds to realize, hey, we have to fill up our gunnysack with these guys. Bending over into the flying sand, with the gunnysack between us, we scooped handfuls of flopping fish into the sack. In less than thirty seconds we had half a sack full and realized we had all we could carry. We dragged the sack further up from the shore and turned around and watched in the dim moonlight this spectacle of spawning fish. Maybe there were millions of them. Us two guys were covered with sand from head to foot. We had to brush, shake, comb, and stomp to get that sand out of our hair and out of our shorts. My friend took the half gunny sack of fish home. He said his mom knew several people who would fry, pickle, or prepare them some other way. I was never around to taste a grunion either.

It was at Seal Beach that we had several memorable beach parties. We would always build a fire and get several big pieces of wood burning good. It would provide some heat, as it gets cool at night down by the ocean. We would have marshmallows to roast, potato chips, soft drinks, and sometimes some beer and blankets to lie on. It wasn't always the same people, but usually about six of us and the same number of girls. We weren't on dates or anything, but would just sort of pair up, if you wanted to, and do some necking. It was a good time for inexperienced teenagers to practice up on their French kissing.

I got paired up one night with a little blonde that was kind of aggressive and we were practicing up all right. All of a sudden she applied a huge vacuum to my tongue and sucked the whole thing into her mouth. I was locked there in a love embrace that was indescribable. It was such a wonderful first time sensation that I just loved her for doing it! When she let me go, I whispered to her, "That was really neat. Let me do that to you." And she did!

In 1948, gasoline in California was seventeen cents a gallon. After all, they made it right there. And leave it to forward-moving California, they had self-service gas stations! With gas so reasonable, it helped people go places and do things. There wasn't any Disneyland yet, but they had Knott's Berry Farm in Anaheim.

Perhaps Knott's main attraction was their farm-raised delicious fried chicken. They had a fine large restaurant that was packed a lot of the time. After dinner came the berry pies with real, old-fashioned, rich ice cream. The whole dinner was hard to beat. On the grounds of the farm they had all kinds of "olden days" stuff to fascinate and entertain you. These ideas were virgin, original, and unique for their time.

They had old-time buildings and shacks that you could look into through windows and see lifelike dummies in perfect character. There was the barbershop where the barber was brandishing a straight edge razor and the customer getting a shave was so apprehensive his hair was standing straight up. There was the saloon that was filled with saloon girls and six-gun toting miners and cowboys. All kinds of shenanigans and card cheating were going on in there. There was the Western graveyard called Boot Hill. There was a very real-looking underground gold mine where you could pan for real gold nuggets. There was a real smoke-belching, steam engine with a half dozen cars that circled the grounds. While you were on board, there would be a train robbery with kerchiefed bandits firing blanks in their six shooters. There was the neat little theater where semiprofessional actors would put on skits and plays where you could participate by hissing and booing the villain that was harassing the damsel in distress and hooray and applaud the rescuing hero. Stage settings and costumes were magnificent. All this was great stuff in 1948. Californians and tourists loved Knott's Berry Farm.

Out on North Long Beach Boulevard, there was a state-of-the-art miniature golf course. It was called Shady Acres. Maybe it was one of the first in the world. It was a serious combination of engineering and architecture resulting in a nine-hole beauty. Playing on it was such fun. The fairways were banked and humped and covered with green material like you would find on a pool table. There was precision throughout. There was the turning windmill blades crossing the fairway you had to shoot down and other trick holes with shortcuts if you felt you were good enough. Uphill and downhill and doglegs—it had it all.

In California, you can grow lush stuff of all kinds. The landscaping and setting at Shady Acres was simply beautiful. This was part of the reason it was so enjoyable. Lush flowers, rocks, trees, and plants perfectly manicured with lighting at night added to the excitement. This little golf course was another popular place in 1948.

My sister Elaine was hooked on horse racing. Racetracks like Hollywood Park and Santa Anita had pretty landscaping and were exciting to go to. My sister went so often that she got to know the tipsters that would set up a small booth or stand outside the main gate and sell forms marked with their predicted winners for each of the day's races. She would always buy one or two. Some of the most famous jockeys like Eddie Arcaro and Willie Shoemaker and some of the Kentucky Derby winners were part of the excitement of the thundering hooves. There were big purses to be won and movie stars in attendance. It was always fun. Betting was something you had to learn. Win, place, or show was about all I could handle. My sister often played the daily double where you had to pick the winners of the first two races to be in the money. She also bet more complicated pari-mutual offerings. My sister lost too much money at the racetracks, which were a red-hot place to gamble. But, they really provided entertainment too. Gambling in all of its forms has been a way of human behavior since day one. When they find ivory dice from

1500 B.C., you know it's true. Las Vegas and the stock market are still carrying on

There was a smaller restaurant in Long Beach called the Rancho. Us three guys ate hundreds of chiliburgers there. Mmm, they were good. They consisted of a large open-face bun with a large hamburger patty on one side and both sides generously smothered with homemade chili loaded with beans, onions, and tomatoes. I always had a malted milk to go with it. And we devoured hundreds of malted milks out on North Long Beach Boulevard at the Clock drive-in. They had cute girls taking your order at the car windows and people visiting from car to car at this popular, always crowded drive-in. What happened to the always-delicious thick malted milks that we ate at the malt shop, the drug store fountain, and at restaurants? They were made with your favorite flavor of rich ice cream and whole milk and a teaspoon of malt and we thrived on them. The malt that went into a malted-milk gave it the 1950s Elvis Presley pizzazz. Malt for malted milks was a dissolvable powder made from dried milk and ground grains like barley. When prohibition outlawed the making of beer and liquor, breweries like Coors Beer in Colorado switched to making prepared malt for malted milks, candies, and things like that just to stay in business. So everyone, including the Borden Company, was making prepared malt and that was one of the reasons it was so widely used. Anyway, we loved it and it was good for you. Today, the distinctly flavored malted milk seems to be extinct.

It was fun to go up to Hollywood. It was new and beautiful too. There was the famous corner of Hollywood and Vine and fancy restaurants like Ciros, The Brown Derby, and the Coconut Grove. There were the exclusive shops of the rich, the Palladium dance hall where Glenn

Miller played, and Grauman's Chinese Theater with the stars in the sidewalk along the Walk of Fame. The Walk of Fame was getting a good start in 1948. One night, us three guys went up to Hollywood in Henry's Model A Ford that he had bought on a whim, and stood at the entrance to the Annual Photographers Ball and ogled the celebrities. The women would emerge from their expensive cars in beautiful off the shoulder, floor length gowns. Their escorts were in tuxedos. The valet would go park their cars. It was exciting stuff.

In 1946, my parents thought they had a good enough car and enough money to make a trip to California from Nebraska. Once we got there, we would stay with my three sisters. So, with my brother and I, the four of us set off for California. We had a used 1937 four-door Oldsmobile with an eight cylinder flathead engine in it. That engine was powerful and absolutely vibration free and General Motors used it for years. The whole car was really nice for its time. Its stick shift was on the floor of course, and then it was about ten years old with lots of miles on it. Dad had managed to buy some wartime synthetic rubber tires to make the trip in. He really worried about the darn things because they had a reputation for flying apart.

Someone had told Dad to let out the extra air pressure that would build up from the heat once you got on the road. So, every morning we would drive about twenty miles and then get out and let four to five pounds of air out of the tires. Holy cow. In the morning the next day, when we got ready to go, the tires would be visibly low. So, we would pump them up, drive twenty miles, and let four to five pounds of air out of each tire. This is the way we went to California. Wartime ingenuity?

I had turned sixteen in 1946, so I had just gotten my drivers license. This made it legal for me to help Dad drive on this trip to California. The only problem was my driving experience consisted of driving up to the icehouse and getting a fifty-pound block of ice put on the bumper and driving home with it. The ice was for our icebox in the kitchen. Therefore, on the trip, I was only allowed to drive where the road was pretty straight and maybe for a half hour at a time. The folks were more worried about my driving than they were about the tires. I was too! To edge that big Oldsmobile up toward fifty miles per hour made my palms sweat and I never took my eyes off the road nor did I move my head a fraction of an inch one way or the other. When I stopped to let Dad take over, I think my tense neck muscles actually cracked as I got out from behind the wheel. Dad never drove faster than fifty miles per hour either. The highways were narrow and constantly winding around something. In the mountains of Colorado and Utah the switchbacks were tight with no guardrails and over the side was straight down.

It was scary in more than one place! Because of all this, we had to put in ten to twelve hour days to get anywhere. The highlight of this trip was when my sisters and all of us went up to Hollywood to see Ken Murray's Blackouts. This was a professional dancing revue with some comedy skits between dance routines. With some abbreviated costumes and shady jokes, the show was on the risqué side for 1946. The costuming was brilliantly flowing as well as the dancing and full orchestra. Ken Murray, a comedian and actor himself, was playing to a packed house for every performance. He had a gold mine right in the middle of town. Right in the middle of a dance routine, I decided

I really needed to go pee. So, I squeezed past the seated people and headed for the men's room.

With the show going on, the restroom was empty and I headed for one of two urinals. I was just getting underway as this huge frame of a man filled the whole area around the other urinal. I looked over and up and my God, it was Sidney Greenstreet! Now you just don't mistake seeing Sidney Greenstreet because he's in *The Maltese Falcon* and because he's a friend of Peter Lorre and because these two guys can be unsavory mean characters. It seemed a bit scary being next to this big man. And being shy, it just wasn't in me to say, "Pleased to meet you, sir," or "Aren't you so and so?" So, I glanced at him at least four more times as I was washing my hands and thinking since I was the first one in the restroom I guess I should be the first one to leave. So, I left. But, what an honor, to take a leak beside Sidney Greenstreet. He was an Englishman and was really large at about 360 pounds. He was also Humphrey Bogart's buddy and costar in some memorable movies of the 1940s. I love a mystery.

But, back to the good times of 1948, 1949, and 1950. With my two good friends, my sisters, and their families, it was a nice time in my life. Off and on my sisters got after me about my bad habit of reaching down with my left hand and pulling up my crotch. They, of course, didn't know why I did it and I didn't really realize that I had a legitimate reason for doing it. But, I did. I got this dull ache in my left scrotum because of some varicose veins in there that trapped the flow of blood. This could become a dull ache if I was on my feet all day and didn't have on good fitting jockey shorts. I just figured it was something men have, so I didn't give it much thought. My friends and I continued on with our fun. Drinking the locally brewed Acme beer, going to movies, playing snooker, bowling, riding the Cyclone roller coaster at the Pike Amusement Park, and going to the big Los Angeles County Fair in the fall out at the town of Pomona.

That fair was beyond my imagination. Gigantic, fun, and crowded, California never ceased to amaze me. We even went to the Rose Bowl in Pasadena. It was the Junior Rose Bowl. It was in December of 1950 and was the junior college football championship of the whole country. It pitted Long Beach Junior College against Boise, Idaho Junior College. Long Beach won 33 to 13. The Junior Rose Bowl was discontinued around 1965.

Then came 16 December 1950 and I became twenty-one years old. This is a big event in a person's life, because you can legally buy beer and vote and all that grown up stuff. My two friends and some girls gave me a really nice birthday party with cake and a couple presents. Of course, there was booze and they kept encouraging me to drink up on this special occasion. As night fell we all left the apartment and drove up to the top of Signal Hill to continue our partying. Overlooking beautiful Long Beach I finally drank so much I teeter-tottered just like the oil wells. I couldn't walk without falling down. The party was over! My friends took care of me, sobered me up, and took me home. I never ever got that way again! The party was over in more ways than one. In December, I had received a notice that I had been drafted into the United States Army for a period of two years and that on 17 January 1951, I was to report to the Los Angeles Civic Center for swearing in ceremonies.

Posting billboards in Long Beach, CA—July '48-'50.

Yea, though I walk through the valley of the shadow of death, I will fear no evil. The little bible given to me by the pastor and choir. I carried it in Korea. It was wet many times.

DRAFTED

Telling the manager at Foster and Kleiser that I had been drafted was kind of hard, because it was my first good job. I showed him my draft notice. He knew that young men were being drafted and that federal law dictated that the draftee's job must be saved for him and that about five percent of his wages must be put in his bank account while he was gone. This money would be tax deductible for the company. He wished me good luck and thanked me for doing a good job.

During the last time I was at church, Reverend Perry came up to me and handed me this little Bible and said, "We wanted you to have this to take with you." He had opened the front cover as he handed it to me. Inside was written, "As a token of esteem to Dan Rasmussen from the Chapel Choir of Good Shepherd Lutheran Church. John H. Perry, Pastor, January 14, 1951." I was surprised and had kind of a happy look as I shook his hand and said, "This is really very nice of you." He smiled back and said, "Be careful and God bless you." Now, I didn't even know what esteem meant, but it sounded special! The dictionary says that esteem means to have a favorable opinion of, or to value highly, or to hold in high regard. Anyway, that was the first and last time I was ever held in esteem. Maybe, in a very small way, I helped hold that small choir together as the church struggled, even though I was a poor note reader. I carried that small Bible for a year in Korea. I still have it. It was wet so many times that the binding is broken, the ink is smeared, and mildew blots the covers.

My sister, Dorothy, and Paul took me up to the army induction place at the Civic Center in Los Angeles. It was 17 January 1951. About five hundred young men began filling up this large hall. We all held up our right hand and were all sworn into the army and pledged to honor our country. Then came our first short-arm inspection.

We were all ordered to drop our pants and pull down our shorts, as about a dozen doctors would be going down the long lines and milking down our peters looking for gonorrhea discharge and maybe worse things. This was a common routine thing in the service, as some of this stuff could be spread. This inspection had just started when this guy standing six guys from me was pulled from the line. Holy God! His scrotum was hanging down to his knees. This guy's condition was just unbelievable!

We were in the front row and there was this table right out in front of me. A couple of doctors had him come forward and as he walked he had to straddle the huge mass of veins that was hanging between his legs. The two doctors picked up this big mass in their hands, laid it on the table, and spread it out. They called out to the other doctors to come up to the front. So, right in front of me, there's a dozen doctors looking at this guy's nuts and shaking their heads. There had to be two pints of blood trapped in this guy's sack. This was the second time that I have seen this condition and I was beginning to wonder if possibly I could have the beginning of this elephantiasis disease. Jesus!

What this guy had was not elephantiasis. It's a condition that twenty percent of all men on earth have. It's something that one out of every five men is walking around with. After talking to doctors and reading up on this, the condition is rarely as bad as this guy's calamity. Most men have a small problem that they live with all their lives and never have anything done about it. This disorder is called a varicocele. It's an abnormal bunch of twisted veins that expand down into the scrotum and really feel like a bag of worms. It's something like varicose veins in the legs. This problem almost always occurs in the left testicle part of the scrotum. The reason for this is the manner in which the return blood leaves the left side. The blood doesn't have a direct dump, like the right side does. It has a detour.

If this detour is more restrictive than normal, it causes more than normal back pressure. This makes the darn veins pool the blood, which in turn leads to the development of the varicocele condition. These engorged veins can also cause higher temperatures in the left side, which can lower sperm production of the testicle and even cause a withering of it to a smaller size. Approximately forty percent of infertile men have a varicocele. The glob of veins can screw up the whole temperature control system of the scrotum. It has been estimated that a sperm can take three months to process through to maturity. The scrotum has a big job of controlling the temperature of the family jewels during this time. Good sperm production requires that the testicles be at a temperature a couple degrees below the mean 98.6 degrees Fahrenheit of the body. The scrotum is made up of muscle fibers that can raise or lower the testicles two to three inches to accomplish this task. Only the experts know where the thermostat is that turns these muscle fibers on and off. It's really an involuntary happening.

Unless a varicocele is supported, the mere weight of the engorged veins causes them to stretch and become bigger and bigger, and heavier and heavier, and causes that dull ache in your crotch. A good fitting pair of jockeys will usually control the problem. I think the varicocele condition that so many men have is still in the closet. Like breast cancer, if it were openly talked about there could be peace of mind for men who are too embarrassed to talk about it. The bad veins can be removed surgically through a small incision if they become too large or are causing infertility. It is not a serious procedure. Other veins take up the job of nourishing the testicle. I have to mention that the dirty Wung Hung Lo jokes are no joke at all! I knew nothing of the above as I headed off to basic training.

The army loaded us all onto a passenger train in Los Angeles. This train even had a few Pullman cars on it with bunk beds to sleep in. I was one of the lucky ones to get a bunk. Because of my excited state of mind and the jerking and bumping all night long, I didn't sleep much. We were on our way to Fort Ord, which was over two hundred miles north of Los Angeles.

The train got us there real early the next morning. That first day at Fort Ord was spent getting boots and fatigues to wear. Of course, we were immediately introduced to marching in a group: fall in, attention, right face, left face, about face, forward march, to the rear march, double time march, company halt, at ease, and fall out. Our cadreman was kind of neat. He acted like he was conducting an orchestra whenever he marched us somewhere. Instead of saying left right, left right, he'd holler, "Hut, Haut, Hut, Horp," with his mouth looking like a gold fish eating fish food. He taught us some cadence calls right away too. Like, "Your left, your left, you left your wife and twenty-four kids, your left." There were many other cadences that we were taught, a few of them on the dirty side. With a lot of them, the marching guys would answer back to the rhythm of their boots pounding the ground when the cadreman hollered, "Sound off." It was kind of fun and made the monotony and hard work of marching more tolerable. We were marched to the barbershop and all got short crew cuts. We were marched to the infirmary and all got many shots for many reasons. We were marched to the paymaster and sighed up for "Buck Private" pay of about $57 per month. That was about a fourth of what I was making on the outside, but the army was providing room and board, clothing, and medical care. It was also at the paymaster that we signed up for the type of payout of our National Service Life Insurance to our parents in case we were killed. It was a $10,000 policy. A smooth talking army lawyer talked most of us into a yearly payout to our parents of $1000 per year for ten years. This he said, "Would guarantee them an income each year for ten years, which would mean a lot to them." He was only doing his job. There were so many fatalities in the first year of fighting in Korea, that if this thing didn't stop, the lump sum payouts to parents could put a dent in the U.S. Treasury. But, I'm still mad at Uncle Sam. A $10,000 lump sum to my parents was what they should have gotten. This way they could have invested or used the money and not have to wait to have it doled out to them! I don't know why I'm still mad. I didn't even get killed!

We were marched to this large classroom building one morning and we were told we were going to be given an IQ test. They handed out several sheets of statements and problems that would challenge or cover the dumbest to the smartest. They also put out Morse code signals over a loudspeaker system to find the guys who might be used in communications somewhere. I couldn't remember my Morse code from Boy Scouts. Dot-dash was an "A" and dot-dot-dot-dash was a "V" for victory from World War II (. . .—was the "V" for victory all through the war—over and over again). Anyway, we were told our IQs as they had determined them. Mine was ninety-eight. The mean average for a large standardized group is one hundred, so I hung in there pretty close. IQ tests are very controversial and so are lie detector tests! I hoped they didn't want to find out whom to use for cannon fodder. That was not a nice thought!

We were only at Fort Ord for about a week. We were trucked up to Camp Roberts, which was north of Fort Ord. Camp Roberts was fourteen miles north of Paso Robles, California, just off Highway 101. Camp Roberts was closed down after World War II. We were some of the first men sent up there as the camp was reactivated and swung into action. This was desert country, rocky and sandy with sagebrush and a few volunteer trees. We were here for fourteen weeks of basic training preparation for war!

We were assigned to barracks. They were two-story buildings with about twenty-five guys downstairs and about twenty-five guys upstairs sleeping on metal cots. In our barracks, which was part of Company B of the Ninety-Fourth Armor Unit, we had three black guys, about eight Japanese Americans, and about ten Hispanic Americans. All of these guys wound up upstairs along with a few white guys. The rest of us bunked downstairs. Our cadreman was a tall soldier, in good physical shape with the rank of corporal. He acted tough and told us just how things were going to be. He had a room to himself at the end of our barracks. Every so often, he would come out of his room in the evening with a bayonet and show us how tough he was. From about twenty-five feet he could throw that bayonet and stick it into the wall with a loud quivering thud. He never missed! As time went by he let some of us try to stick that bayonet into the wall, but none of us could.

We were quarantined to our barracks for one week and restricted to base for a month. We had gotten our M1 rifle, cartridge belt, and helmet liner. We quickly had a class on the M1 rifle and that was one of the things that better be clean. The whole barracks also had to shine, including the windows and the latrine. On several occasions, when something didn't suit the corporal, we found ourselves out on the parade ground marching till midnight. Or, if your rifle barrel had a little lint in it, you could find yourself standing guard outside the front door till midnight. I must have had a shit-eating grin too much of the time, because one morning when we fell in outside the barracks he wanted to know what I was grinning about. I found myself giving him fifty pushups. And that was before breakfast!

My grin got me into trouble one other time. About three weeks after our arrival there, they put another young black fellow into our barracks. He was either husky and stern looking, or he was husky and shy looking. Anyway, he was bunked across from me and during the first few days I smiled at him a few times, just trying to be friendly. It was on the night of his third day with us that he motioned me over to him and as we kind of huddled around this four by four support timber, he showed me this knife with a five-inch blade. "Sucka," he said, in a blood curdling way, "if y'all don't get off my back, y'all gonna find this knife sticking out of your heart!" I took this seriously. I shook my head from side to side and keeping it quiet I said, "I sure didn't mean anything by what I've been doing. I'll leave you be!" Our eyes parted as I left and got over on my own side. He must have thought I was making fun of him. I mentioned this to no one. In a few more days, he was no longer present in our barracks. Don't know what happened to him. Maybe it was difficult being a black man. The Japanese Americans, Hispanics, and other blacks upstairs were doing fine.

We had a lot of classes on different things as the weeks began to go by. Of course, there was a class or two on discipline and how we were to respect rank and follow orders. There were classes on being AWOL (Absent Without Leave), desertion, and army tactics. There were the classes on specific weapons: how to tear them apart, care for them, and use them. We learned about the M1 rifle, the air-cooled and water cooled .30-caliber machine guns, the .45 pistol, the hand grenade, the bazooka, and the smaller .30-caliber carbine.

We began to take hikes, with our rifle of course, out over the rolling hills and into the desert. All this hiking put muscles on top of your muscles. Calisthenics did too! One day we hiked about seven miles into the desert and were told we would be staying overnight and sleeping on the ground. A couple of army 5x5 trucks arrived with pup tents, sleeping bags, C-rations, and five-gallon cans of water. We buddied up and pitched our tents. And low and behold, we found out the place was crawling with tarantulas. These guys were big and hairy and three to four inches in diameter, counting the legs, and they scared the hell out of you. Of course, we didn't know they seldom bite a human being, but like all spiders, they are poisonous. We spent some free time that afternoon driving those tarantulas out of their homes by pouring water into their holes. The guys killed a lot of them. That night, I either had one of those spiders crawl across my face or I had a vivid dream. In the pitch-blackness of the pup tent, I frantically searched the top of my sleeping bag by lighting book matches that had come with our C-rations. I couldn't find any spiders, but I sure tried to for a while. My dad always said, "If I killed a snake during the day, I would kill him again that night." Guess they brought us out here to tarantula hill to get us used to things to come.

Another hike we took was a fourteen-mile forced march out into the desert and back. We got back about mid-afternoon that day. There had been a great deal of limping and moaning and groaning the last few miles. We were on the outskirts of the barracks area when we were told, "The death march is over. Take a break and in about ten minutes there will be a map reading exercise for those of you that are interested." Most of the guys immediately ripped off their boots to look at their feet, me included. Some guys had silver dollar-sized blisters and bleeding around their toenails. I didn't have either of these problems, but both of my feet were so sore I didn't want to take another step on them! "Okay you guys," our corporal barked, "map readers congregate by that tree over there." He was pointing to a tree fifty yards away. It seemed like, to most of us, that that tree was fifty miles away and we wouldn't be able to make the trip. About ten guys did hop up and the rest of us watched as they went there and yonder doing what the maps and compasses told 'em. With some admiration I thought to myself, "Maybe those guys have what it takes to be leaders." Half the barracks fell out for sick call the next morning, including me. Most guys' feet were still sore the next morning and weren't really ready for marching too far. Combat boots ain't exactly Florsheim Hush Puppies. "Your heels do stick out back a little further than normal," the doctor told me at sick call. "Otherwise, your feet really seem to be in good shape." He seemed to be a nice honest doctor who was probably drafted just like me and would spend part of his internship in Korea.

As far as I was concerned, the food in the army was generally great. And that included shit on a shingle. A lot of guys wouldn't agree with me. I suppose the army used powdered eggs and dehydrated potatoes, but it didn't seem like the mess halls were preparing that stuff for us. When they work you hard, you're starved, and anything tastes good and you want plenty of it. I would finish everything they threw on my tray and then head over to the exit door of the mess hall where there were always a couple gallon cans of jelly sitting there with thick slices of fresh army baked bread. Not being a fast eater and going for the extra jelly bread grub, I was always one of the last guys out of the mess hall. I guess that's why I finally filled out my six-foot frame and went to 170 pounds. None of us pulled KP duty in the kitchen while we were going through our fourteen weeks of basic training.

With all of us guys sleeping and eating and training together twenty-four hours a day, we got to know each other pretty well. I think all eight of the Japanese Americans upstairs in our barracks had had some training in ju-jitsu, especially this one fellow. I don't remember his name, but he was supposed to have a black belt or whatever they awarded for the best in that type of martial arts in those days. Ju-jitsu is a variant of Judo and uses the weight and strength of an opponent against himself. Using surprise, quickness, unbalance, and leverage, an expert can have you in trouble in a hurry. It was always while waiting in our chow line, that we kept asking the black belt to show us something. It was one of those chow line days when I said to him, "Is today the day you're going to show us one of the things you can do?" "Yeah, yeah," a couple other guys eagerly said, "show us something." The words had hardly left their mouths when I found myself flying through the air. The black belt pulled up on my arm to break my fall as I landed flat on my back on the desert ground. There were mostly open mouths and wide eyes as I turned over and got to my feet. I wasn't hurt, but I could see that I might have been! There were some oohs and aahs and a few "Did you see that?" comments. We never bugged him again to show us something. I knew I would dread going up against him in hand-to-hand combat.

We had been hitting the firing range right along. We were getting quite a bit of practice with our M1 rifles, standing, sitting, and in the prone position. We were taught how to wrap the wed belt around our arm for better firing stability. Fresh targets were run up in the firing pits. There were some red Maggie's drawers run up when the guys would miss the target completely. Most of the time it was hard to tell how well you did because of the distance we were firing at. The NCOs had field glasses and worked their way up and down the line. Then you would be told how many bull's-eyes you didn't get. I wasn't totally green at this because back home my dad had a .22-caliber rifle, a 410, and a 12-gauge shotguns. My brother and I got some practice with these guns shooting rabbits and hunting pheasant. My brother was a much better shot than I was. On this army firing range, we had no ear protection when we were shooting all this stuff. Some people's ears are more sensitive to noise damage than others. I must have been one of them. The M1 rifle left my ears ringing, but the couple different days we fired the .30-caliber air-cooled and water-cooled machine guns I was practically deaf. Back at the barracks those evenings, the guys would have to holler into my ears to tell me what we were supposed to do. I don't know if I suffered permanent hearing damage or not. You're not aware of a slight change and there was not a routine hearing test conducted by the army in those days.

It was kind of fun firing the .45-caliber pistol. That's a pretty heavy gun that fires a big slug and kicks a good amount. The targets were closer, so you could see where your rounds were going. I'm not sure why we got to fire the .45 because only the officers carried them. Not everyone got to fire the bazooka, but I was buddied up with a guy and told to hold the tube on my shoulder. He got behind me and loaded a bazooka round. I was suppose to aim it into the hillside out front and to pull the trigger, which I did. The dirt flew as the round exploded against the hill thirty yards out. There wasn't any kick or much noise as all of that went out the back of the tube. I think this was the smaller, less effective bazooka used in World War II.

The hand grenade was the last explosive device we handled. We all got to throw a live one. The hand grenade seemed to me to be the scariest weapon of them all. The guys stood in line about a hundred and fifty feet from where an NCO was taking us one at a time. Having never seen a grenade other than in the movies, or held one, made you pay attention to what he was saying. "First of all, you grab the grenade so your thumb is around this handle and your four fingers are around the body of the grenade. You'll then pull this ring, which pulls the pin out and arms the grenade. The timed fuse will not start until the handle under your thumb is released. You'll be releasing the handle as you throw it. You will throw it over this dirt wall and it will explode down in the ravine on the other side of the wall where it won't hurt anyone. Any questions?" The NCO was watching you like a hawk as you did what you had just been told. He was watching for the guy that might panic and just drop it. That would give him a couple seconds to gather it up and get it over the wall. Grenades had a fuse of about four and a half seconds. Our exploding grenades were muffled and out of sight in the ravine. This didn't really let you see the damn thing go off and again you wondered what it would really be like if you were close enough to someone to throw a grenade and try and kill 'em!

The infiltration course was next on their program. In a very serious, storytelling loud voice, the NCO got our attention. "During World War II, when the guys were going through this course, one soldier was killed!" There was a pause as he scanned each and every one of us. "That morning as this guy was crawling along on his belly, he came face to face with a large rattlesnake. The coiled snake, with his flicking tongue, made him lose his senses and he jumped to his feet. The machine guns mowed him down, deader than the snake would have ever made him. You better remember this is live ammunition we are shooting about three feet over your head, so stay on the ground. And stay out of the shell craters, as they may have a surprise you won't want to experience. You can readily see how to crawl ahead under, and I said under, the obstacles and barbwire. Are there any questions?" We had done some crawling on our toes and knees and elbows with our bellies flat on the ground, so we knew how to do that. Your rifle was usually in your hands out front, sometimes cradled in your elbows. So off we went as the machine guns began to chatter. They had set some dynamite charges in the shell crater holes. When they were detonated they were loud and would shower dirt down on you. It was pretty realistic, but you pretty much knew you weren't going to get hurt. We had to crawl about seventy-five feet. It didn't take too long. And again, you wondered, "Man, what will it really be like?"

We spent most of a day at the bayonet practice area. We were given a bayonet and scabbard to hook onto our cartridge belt. NCOs worked with us. They showed us how to hook the bayonet to the end of the rifle and showed us some footwork as we plunged our bayonets into the bales of hay again and again. They kept hollering, "Hit 'em hard! Only a doctor knows how tough a human body is. Hit 'em hard!" An equally impressive defensive move they showed us that day was the rifle butt as a weapon. With your left hand up by the barrel, it becomes the pivot point. Your right hand, on the upper part of the gunstock, brings the butt end across your opponent. With that nine-pound rifle, wicked force can be generated.

We saw our first tanks one day. We skirmished with a couple of World War II Sherman tanks. Another day, groups of four spent five minutes with an expert and his 60-millimeter mortar. He threw a little trigonometry at you and turned some dials and hollered, "Next!" I didn't understand a thing about it! Another day, this shack inside was cloudy with tear gas. One after the other, we donned a gas mask and had to enter the shack. It was hard to see in there, but didn't seem too bad until two steps from the exit door you had to take off your mask. God, that stuff was bitter and burning. You got the hell out of there in a hurry. When you think back on all the stuff we did in basic training, you had to say that Uncle Sam was doing a fair job in fourteen weeks.

After the sixth week of basic training, we were allowed to leave Camp Roberts at noon on Saturdays for the weekend. We had to be back on base by midnight Sunday. This guy from Long Beach went home the first weekend certainly nothing serious. Just a few enlarged veins. They could be removed some day if they get larger and bother you. What I am going to do is give you a suspensory to take with you and use if you feel the need." A suspensory is like a jock strap only it just goes around your waist and has a hole for your dong.

So, at noon, on Saturday, 5 May 1951, we all graduated from basic training as Privates First Class. We were released from the base on 10 May and had a fourteen-day leave with orders to report to Camp Stoneman, which was an embark/debarkation camp near San Francisco.

SAN FRANCISCO TO YOKOHAMA

It took about a day and a half to get to Long Beach, from Camp Roberts, and get on a train to Nebraska. With two days on the train to Grand Island, three and a half days of my fourteen were already gone. It would be another three and a half days back to Camp Stoneman, so I only had seven days at home. Mom and Dad, of course, were glad to see me and I was happy to see them. I spent a couple of days looking up old school friends and the rest of the time was spent with Mom and Dad. I did see my married younger brother and his new wife. Then it was back to the train depot. It was tough saying good-bye. I don't know just what the folks really thought about what might be ahead. I know Mom went home and put a 78 rpm record away. No one was to play it until I got home. It had on it the cowboy song of "Cool Water" sung by the Sons of the Pioneers. It was a song that I liked.

It seemed different when the train didn't branch off at Salt Lake City and head for Los Angeles. It was going to be different being in San Francisco too, as I had never been there. As it turned out, we were at Camp Stoneman for ten days. It takes time to accumulate a couple thousand guys for overseas shipment. We were given a couple one-day passes, so different small groups of us got over to downtown San Francisco and went sightseeing. We went to the Top Of The Mark Hotel, which was a treat. I don't know if it was the tallest building in Frisco, but a stunning view of the famous harbor was before your eyes. The Golden Gate and the Oakland Bay Bridge and Alcatraz were just part of the scenery. I'm sure there were some famous criminals out on the Alcatraz rock.

The sightseeing and hanging around came to an abrupt halt when I was snagged for KP (kitchen police) duty. And it was a bummer. The duty roster glared out, "The following men will report to the mess hall at 0400." The mess hall sergeant blurted out, "You're mine for the next sixteen hours and I want all your dog tags. You better still be here when I give them back late tonight! Right now, we're going to feed you breakfast and then you are going to work!" He was talking to a bunch of us. We ate well and then it was repeated three times that day. In huge sinks, we washed huge pots and pans, washed trays, cups and utensils, and out in a lean-to we peeled potatoes. You never really got done before it started all over again. It was a big job cleaning that big mess hall too.

The ten days were over and it was time for us to head out to sea. Early in the morning we boarded smaller transport craft at Camp Stoneman. At the Stoneman dock there was a small group of people, mostly women, and a small band waving flags and banners and bidding us farewell. The transports headed over to Frisco harbor. Boy, now you could really see the Golden Gate Bridge and Alcatraz and then, there was the big ship. The *General C.G. Morton* was going to be our home for a couple of weeks. Loading of that big rascal went on all day. By suppertime there were about 1700 of us army soldiers on board. We were herded down the stairwells and told where we were going to bunk. I remember getting the sleeper on the train out of Los Angeles and never expected to be that lucky again, but I was. Another guy and I were given this small two-bunk stateroom, and a toilet was right down the hall. What a break! Almost all the guys ended up down in the bowels of the ship in these huge rooms. Their bunks were stacked six high along the walls. It wasn't exactly the Ritz for these guys. A lieutenant came around and told us, "We are on a fourteen-day trip to Yokohama, Japan. Keep plenty of food on your stomach and you won't get seasick." So, in the galley of the ship that night, I ate all the stuff on my tray. The main part of the meal was roast beef and black-eyed peas.

It was 4 June 1951, and as the sun was beginning to sink in the sky, the anchor on the *General Morton* was raised and we began to move. We were all up on deck. It was kind of a momentous occasion for us. There are strong currents in Frisco Bay and the strong afternoon winds were coming in off the ocean. The *General Morton* began to slowly and gently rock back and forth and spent a half hour getting herself under the Golden Gate Bridge and underway. I wasn't the first one to get seasick. There were dozens of us guys running to the railing and heaving our guts out. The roast beef and black-eyed peas were flying all over the place. The wind would catch the goop and throw it right back in your face. And, it wasn't necessarily your own goop. It was lousy. We were seasick and we hadn't even cleared the Golden Gate Bridge and hit the real ocean.

On the first day out to sea, our little stateroom went public. Maybe my bunk buddy knew somebody down in the hold and the word spread. Anyway, during the days ahead, there were up to a half dozen guys in our room most of the time during the day. I hadn't told anyone. We were all strangers. The guys that came up brought cards and books, so there was some card playing and laughter. All of a sudden there were at least a half dozen Mickey Spillane paperback mysteries floating around. I love a mystery. So, I lay up in my top bunk and went through, *I The Jury*, *My Gun Is Quick*, and *Vengeance Is Mine*. Mickey Spillane's Mike Hammer was a cool cucumber. We got the word one of those first nights that they were going to show the movie *Samson and Delilah*, with Victor Mature, up on deck. Come show time, it was drizzling a little. I had seen it anyway, and I was in the middle of Spillane's *My Gun Is Quick*, so I didn't even go up. It was the only movie that they showed on our two-week trip.

It was on the second day out that I made a trip down into the hold. You wouldn't believe it! I couldn't believe what I was seeing. There was women's lingerie hanging all over the place. There were panties, brassieres, girdles, corsets, garter belts, nylons, slips, and nighties displayed all over the hold. They were even hanging from six bunks up. It was wonderful. These guys had wives and sweethearts back home and this was just a way of staying in contact with them for a little while longer. It wasn't easy for any of them to interrupt their lives and donate two years to Uncle Sam. I think most of us on this ship were drafted. Anyway, I quickly thought of Marlene. Gosh, I wished I had a pair of Marlene's panties. I didn't' feel embarrassed or out of line anymore. I was just one of the guys.

Four days out of Frisco, the smart-ass swabbies took advantage of our ignorance. We were all notified that during the next day we would be crossing the 180th meridian and that there was a buoy anchored there that served as a mailbox so this would be a good way to get a letter off to people back home as the next ship going back would stop and pick up the letters. It was pen and pencil time. I think almost all of us sat down and wrote at least one letter if not two or three. Well, there wasn't any buoy that served as a mailbox. We were tricked. But, I think this spoof was an accepted practice by higher-ups. It encouraged reluctant letter writers to sit down and jot down a little to the concerned or worried people back home. Hey, from here on out we had free postage. You just write "Free Mail" up where the stamp would go. We all put our letters in the ship's mail system. They mailed them for us in Yokohama.

I was only seasick that first night leaving San Francisco. Being way out on the blue Pacific like this was something I never thought of happening. We weren't on a luxury liner, but it sure was interesting. They had a small PX and a small library on board. I just looked in the doors. They weren't exactly meant for us troops. One early evening we hit some really rough seas. We were confined below decks. The ship was heaving fore and aft so much that the screw came out of the water a couple of times and sent a slight shudder through the ship. The rough condition didn't last long. We would have a routine inspection about every three days. Nothing serious. The officers would make the rounds and wanted your bunk made up that day. On 16 June, in late afternoon, it was land ahoy. Japan and Yokohama Harbor were straight ahead. Again we were all up on deck taking in the docking at this strange place.

With a hold full of lingerie!

Fox Company gathered around our commander in Korea.

YOKOHAMA TO FOX COMPANY

We spent our last night on board the troop ship. For those down in the hold, it had to be a pleasant expectation after fourteen days on the high seas. But all of us would probably be staying in worse places in the days to come. In the army, transporting men from here to there was most often done in the back of a stake truck. These trucks could hold a couple dozen guys sitting on folding benches. So after our last breakfast aboard ship, we were trucked to a Japanese train station. A good crowd of Japanese people cheered and waved at us as we pulled away from the station in this small windowless train. Guess they were glad to see us. The train took us out to a former Jap officers' training camp. There were alot of Japanese people working in and around this camp. At the camp the U.S. army was busy posting different assignments for us guys. In two days I was back on another train heading South. This train was small too, but had windows and was clean, neat, and again was driven by a steam engine. The seats were small too, as Japanese people were not very big. All these trains ran on a narrow gauge railroad system. The train was just getting outside of the Tokyo area. For some reason, I've always remembered this Japanese rice farmer standing in his rice paddy taking a leak. He was about a hundred feet from the train, ankle deep in water, and had on his round coolie hat. He was doing his thing like we weren't even there. That was funny. Guess he was kind of the first Japanese civilian I had seen in his natural habitat. The Japanese had what Americans called the honey pots system. They collected human waste and used it on their fruits and vegetables. We were told that Japanese fruits and vegetables could upset our digestive systems. They did grow some nice ones.

In a short while, Mt. Fuji started to loom in the distance. Mt. Fuji is a pretty sight. At 12,400 feet and snowcapped, it is one of the most majestic and symbolic things in Japan. In centuries past, this symmetrically formed, cone-shaped volcanic mountain had been worshipped and feared as a god. The ancient Shinto religion worshipped objects like mountains and seas and symbolic objects like swords. They thought such things were inhabited by spirits and must be appeased.

When reflecting on volcanoes, you might say that Japan had an equivalent to the hydrogen bomb go off in 1707. That's when Mt. Fuji last exploded. Since that's been almost three hundred years ago, Fuji can be classified as pretty much dormant. But, with a mighty blast that day, it buried Tokyo, about eighty miles away, in six inches of ash. There must have been much fear and worshipping that day. Mt. Fuji and Mt. Saint Helens in Washington State are of the same kind of volcanoes. They tend to spew volcanic debris out their tops with a gigantic blast, as compared to volcanoes that gurgle lava over their top and down their sides. Mt. Saint Helens blew its top at 8:32 in the morning of 18 May 1980 with a megaton blast of superheated gases and volcanic debris. The stuff was propelled out its topside at speeds of two hundred miles per hour. In seconds, the velocity and heat stripped the bark from the dense stand of mountain fir trees, then momentarily set them on fire, and then blew them over like toothpicks. Like Tokyo, Yakima, Washington was covered in ash. It wasn't six inches deep like in Tokyo, but in the northwest part of Yakima it was an inch deep and generally it was three quarters of an inch deep throughout the city. The ash made it look like nightfall, causing all the streetlights to come on. All rooftops were the first thing that had to be cleaned, as you couldn't have the ash coming down again as the wind blew. It was estimated that 600,000 tons of ash fell within the Yakima city limits. The cost of cleanup was about three million dollars and went on for years. I now live 140 miles due east of Mt. Saint Helens in the state of Washington. We were on the fringe of the major ash cloud on that eruption day. You couldn't quite feel the ash hit your face as it floated to the ground. It was coming down out of what looked like giant udders in the sky. Of course they were gray in color and the tips of them that were hanging down were closer to black.

It had to be the heat and the gas that was still in the ash cloud that made them sort of float in the air in these weird udder shapes. I think the nipples of these udders were blacker in color because the heavier ash particles were being drawn down by the earth's gravity. The ash cloud left 3/32 of an inch of Mt. Saint Helens on our driveway. I swept some of it up and put it in a baby jar. It was just like flour. Then I hosed down the driveway and encouraged it to flow down the gutter of the street. The next morning I looked at ash still in the gutter. I swept some up and put it in another baby jar. It was darker and coarser. The finer particles had washed away leaving the heavier coarse stuff. Months later, we visited the blast zone of Mt. Saint Helens. The tour guide took us up on private lumber company back roads. We could see the 240 square miles of ruined toothpicks and canyons completely filled with ash. Some articles say a blast comparable to fifty megatons of TNT went off. That's like two twenty-megaton hydrogen bombs. Hiroshima's atomic bomb was approximately twenty thousand tons of TNT. So, the Mt. Saint Helens blast was 2,500 times more powerful than the atomic bomb dropped on Hiroshima. They say that Mt. Rainier, which is about fifty miles north of Mt. Saint Helens, is the most dangerous volcano in the United States. Mt. Rainier had an eruption in 1870 that was mildly severe.

Volcanic activity is so in evidence here in the Pacific Northwest. There is basalt everywhere. Basalt rock is solidified lava. The sign at the Rye Grass Summit, coming down the east slope of the Cascade Mountains from Seattle, says, "Welling up from within the earth, and rushing across the land, lava flowed out of huge openings and covered tens of thousands of acres, smothering and killing everything in its path. This occurred repeatedly ten to fourteen million years ago." Today, mountain building is still going on. All around the Pacific Ocean rim, two-thirds of approximately four hundred active volcanoes, along with earthquakes, are off and on releasing the anger that lays shallow and deep within the earth.

The mountains that were built in the Cascades of Washington and Oregon and down into California are a work of art. One of the most beautiful drives in the world lays between Biggs, Oregon, on the Columbia River in northern Oregon, and Mt. Shasta in northern California. If you take this 375-mile drive on a cold, crystal clear day, around the first week of March when the mountains are dressed in all their winter snow splendor and are sparkling like diamond snow cones in the brilliant sun, you will see this work of art. There are so many mountain peaks to see on this trip that they can't all be mentioned. But there is a viewpoint, south of Shaniko, Oregon, where you can see thirteen of them at the same time. All of these are about 10,000 feet or higher. To the north in Washington, there is Mt. Rainier at 14,470 feet, and Mt. Adams, and Mt. Saint Helens. Looking down into Oregon, you can see Mt. Hood, Mt. Jefferson, Three Fingers Jack, Mt. Washington, the Three Sisters, and Broken Top. Mt. Shasta, in California, tops 14,000 feet at the end of this trip. Mt. Shasta is spectacular and symmetrical in shape just like Mt. Fuji.

Fifty miles northeast of Mt. Shasta and about twenty miles south of the Oregon border, is a national park called Lava Beds National Monument. At this park there are many lava tubes that you can go down into and explore. These tubes were blown clean at the end of an eruption and remain hollow down into the bowels of the earth. Some of the tube openings are as big as a house. Can you imagine red-hot liquid rock pouring out of the end of your house and spreading across your neighborhood? You can also experience total darkness and claustrophobia down in these tubes. Mt. Saint Helens has a tube on its south side that is over two miles long. They calculate that volcanic activity created it some 2,000 years ago.

Looking back now, out the windows of our troop train, Mt. Fuji was barely visible in the distance as our train pulled up to our first rest stop. There were no toilets on board the train, so we stopped three to four times a day. We had to sleep sitting up in our little seats that first night as the train kept chugging along. We ate a lot of sandwiches passed out by Japanese men. The train kept heading southwest across

Japan. Our destination was a southwest port on the Sea of Japan.

I don't think too many of us realized that down there at the tip of the big island of Honshu, we were about twenty-five miles from Hiroshima. Hiroshima was leveled by the first atomic bomb on 6 August 1945. So, in July of 1951, it was one month shy of being six years since the bomb was dropped. I was just sure that the Japanese were still mad at us and in the back of my mind I felt they couldn't be trusted and I was an intruder in their country. But, quite the opposite was true. General MacArthur had been a master at guiding the occupation of Japan after World War II. He had insisted the Japanese be allowed to keep their emperor and in that way were able to save face. The Emperor, in turn, told the Japanese people to totally accept the occupation and even some of our principles of democracy. It all worked out pretty well for the seven-year term of United States military occupation. Little did I know at this time that I would work for thirty-seven years at the Hanford Nuclear Reservation where some of the material was made for the two atomic bombs dropped on Japan.

It was getting dark on the second day of the train ride when we arrived at the port. About fifteen of us were singled out by an army cadreman and hustled over to this small tug-like boat. He had boarded the tug in front of us and pointing into the interior of the hold he hollered, "Make yourselves at home," and then he left. The tug had a three-man Japanese crew. They started the engines and we were moving out into the darkness. I kind of felt like the United States Army had abandoned us to these three Japs. We all slept on the straw mat that was lining the hold as we chugged across the Sea of Japan on a 125-mile trip to Pusan, Korea. We were tired as there wasn't much sleeping on the train. It was funny that the U.S. would hire this small tug to ferry fifteen of us to Korea. But, this Korean takeover by the communists was such a menace to the world that all stops had been pulled out. Japan was really mobilizing, with the help of U.S. money, to help stop this threatened takeover of Korea and Japan by communist China and Russia.

We docked about daybreak in a harbor at Pusan. We were trucked to a military base near there. In this barracks I was assigned a bunk and given a mess kit. I was just about to sit down on my bunk when someone hollered into the door of the barracks that breakfast chow was ready. There was a clanging of mess kits as the guys grabbed them up and headed for the door. About this time, this kid goes out of his head and starts punching the rough hewed wall of the barracks with his bare fists. He was red in the face and hitting the wall like he was fighting off the devil himself. His knuckles were all bruised and bloodied up before a couple guys got to him and held him. He kind of whimpered as he calmed down. It seemed like he was going to be all right. He must have thought the guy hollering breakfast was hollering incoming artillery and the clanging mess kits were rounds exploding. He was obviously a mental wreck from being shot at too many times. He was heading home, but not in too good a shape. Welcome to Korea!

We had a big breakfast and then at a close by warehouse we got a bunch of stuff. We got an M1 rifle, a pack with a webbed harness, a folding shovel, poncho, canteen, steel helmet and liner, bayonet, and a cartridge belt full of eight round cartridge clips. We had to hook all this stuff together and store and adjust some of it. We also got a large compression bandage in a webbed pouch to hang from our cartridge belt. We then got back onto stake trucks and headed for a train terminal in Pusan. This little train we boarded was something else. It seemed put together with bailing wire, orange crates, and nails. There were no windows in the five little cars and the seats were mostly timber and boards. The whole train looked like it had had it and wasn't up to the task. We were told we would have to stand guard duty for an hour each. Two men were stationed at each end of a car looking out in opposite directions. With loaded rifle in hand, we were told to keep a lookout for Russian MIG airplanes. They had attacked the train in the past. We were headed north on a 175-mile trip to Yongdongpo, where a replacement camp was situated outside of Seoul, Korea. We didn't see any MIGs that day. They stayed up north pretty much that year I was there. The upper part of Korea that lies against China eventually became known as MIG Alley. Frequent encounters between our jets and Russian MIGs took place there. These MIGs could be piloted by North Koreans, Chinese, or Russian pilots. They were all involved.

I spent three nights at this Yongdongpo camp, which was surrounded by barbwire and occupied a somewhat damaged large building in this Seoul suburb. There were no civilians around. It was too dangerous for them to be up this far. In the mornings, again using stake trucks, they would deliver guys to the companies on the front line about twenty miles north of Seoul. The front line was stretched pretty much across the 38th parallel from the east coast to the west coast of Korea. The United Nations forces had just managed to push the Chinese back across the 38th about four to six weeks before I got there. That involved fierce fighting and I was lucky I missed that. The 38th parallel was the division line between North and South Korea set up by an agreement with cantankerous Russia at the end of World War II.

My morning for going to the front line came. I was headed for Fox Company of the Second Battalion of the Thirty-fifth Infantry Division. I think the whole Second Battalion was back in reserve at this time. The Second Battalion is made up of four companies: Easy, Fox, George, and Howe. (Howe Company is a heavy weapons company.) It seemed odd, but I was the only guy getting on the truck to go to Fox Company that morning. Guess they only needed one more man to bring it up to full strength. Anyway, the truck driver told me to ride up front with him. We were headed to somewhere outside Seoul and had been on this dirt road about fifteen minutes, when WHAM, this artillery round makes the dirt fly to our front left, short of the road. The driver slammed on the brakes and hollered at me at the same time, "Get under the truck!"

We got under there in a flash, looking wide-eyed when, WHAM, another round came in. It was a lot closer, but still short of us. There wasn't any shrapnel hitting the truck or kicking up dust real close. We lay there for about ten minutes and when nothing else came in, we hurriedly got back in the truck and tore ass up the road. I don't know just how far away those Chinese were that were trying to knock out our truck. The explosions weren't real big, so they were probably firing a 61mm mortar. They had to be in behind the front line though, and only fired the two rounds to keep from being detected. As I said, the front line was still unstable at this time. When the Chinese retreated a few weeks before, they may have deliberately hid this mortar with a certain number of rounds for it. A Chinese mortar man could sneak across the line at night and pick out a target or two the next day. Then sneak back or hole up with a food supply. They could move the mortar around too, so it would be hard to find. A 61mm mortar doesn't fire that far. It can propel a four-pound shell about a mile. These guys firing at us had to be able to see us, so they could see where their rounds were hitting and make corrections accordingly. They were probably less than a half-mile from us because of this. Infiltration of North Koreans and Chinese was a serious problem throughout the war, as to us these people all looked alike.

The truck driver delivered me to Fox Company. When walking me to the Company CP (command post), we walked past the kitchen mess tent. Close by, this guy was just finishing digging a 6x6. This is a huge square hole in the ground, six feet, by six feet, by six feet. It is a lot of work. You can't even get out when you are finished, unless someone pulls you out by the handle of the shovel. Anyway, this hole would be used to dump garbage in from the mess tent. Someone who screws up, like disobeying an order, often digs it. I really didn't ever want to dig one.

The company commander, a first lieutenant, called us all together and since it was the Fourth of July 1951, he said a prayer for the dead and the missing. I was a replacement. I was a rifleman put in the second squad of the third platoon. I was drafted to come here. Now that I had arrived it wasn't a real great feeling! That night the nine of us in the squad slept on a straw mat floor inside this South Korean farmer's house. Long abandoned by the farmer, the house—thatched roof and all—survived the carnage as the armies marched up and down the country. The city of Seoul changed hands four times in the first year of fighting.

Clouds of volcanic ash from the eruption of Mount St. Helens billow over Richland on May 18, 1980. Richland is about 140 miles from Mount St. Helens and was on the fringe of the very low hanging ash cloud that was moving eastward.

Used with permission of the *Tri City Herald*.

PATROL AFTER PATROL AND TWO OUTPOSTS

I only got to spend that one night in the Korean farmer's thatched roof house, as the very next morning the whole Second Battalion pulled out of reserve and headed for the front line. In doing this, we walked down a deserted side street of the city of Seoul. The street showed the turmoil of war. This street had a single trolley track running down the middle of it, but no trolley. Not much stuff had been lining the sides, but there were a couple of small pagoda-shaped buildings still standing at the end of the street. There were no civilians around. We heard there was a smallpox epidemic putting the city off limits, but again it wasn't safe for civilians to be up this far at this time.

Being a peon groundpounder in the army means a lot of the time you just follow the guy in front of you. You don't really know what is going on. Leaving Seoul, we put in a good day's walk and wound up bivouacking in an area about half a mile behind the front line. This place was going to be our patrol base for the next two and a half months. From the first part of July to the middle of September we went out and we came back. The idea of constantly going out into enemy territory is to keep the enemy off balance and prevent him from building up any kind of large force unseen. For ten weeks we went on daytime and nighttime patrols. They were squad size, platoon size, company size, and two-company size. Most of the time, the whole of Fox Company went out by itself. These patrols were all combat patrols in that we would fight if confronted. The two outposts that they put us out on during this time were the worst part of this seeking out the enemy. When you are sent to an outpost, you are sitting ducks, you're bait, and you're daring the enemy to do something to you.

It was here at our patrol base that I got buddied up with Bob Reusnow. We were both in the third platoon and we shared a pup tent together whenever we were back in the bivouac area. Bob was a James Cagney lookalike. Pug faced and short like Cagney, he could do a great "All right you guys" imitation of him. He did a little "Yankee Doodle Dandy" song and dance too. His dad was a career army officer and Bob, believe it or not, was a little enthusiastic about being in a combat zone.

In 1948, after going to work in California, I had enough money to see a dentist for the first time in my life. I had sixteen cavities filled and a molar pulled. After getting my draft notice, people were telling me, "Get your teeth fixed before you go into the army." They had said, "Army dentists are no good." So, I had gotten a removable one-tooth bridge put into that vacant molar space. And now, going on these patrols, I was also temporarily wearing the suspensory the doctor had given me for my scrotum. Inside our pup tent at night, Bob and I would laugh when I removed all these support parts. He admitted he was lucky to get into the army, as his feet weren't the best in the world. Anyway, he was from Chicago, and he was a dandy, and we became good friends. I think he was my fairy godmother two or three times.

Before we went out on our first patrol, us new guys attended a briefing that mainly covered what to do if you were captured. Believe you me, that is a subject that is on your mind. After seeing all the World War II movies that had actors like Dana Andrews, Pat O'Brian, John Wayne, and all the others, someone was always getting captured and tortured. Your frame of mind for this part of playing soldier was badly warped.

There was a testimonial in a newspaper by a United States Marine who was captured and tortured in a North Korean prison camp in 1952. (Some of our marines wore yellow leggings and the Chinese and North Koreans put a price on their heads. The enemy could get money and a leave for the capture of these marines.) The marine told this story: "At this prison camp they had a hut, made of stone, that was a torture chamber. You are strapped naked on this table with your head blocked, so you can't move it. Drops of salt brine water are aimed to drop on your forehead from a tank overhead. The drops splatter and saturate your face. The water puddles in your eye sockets and leaks through your eyelids and burns and burns, and even burns after your eyes are tightly swollen shut. After hours of this the membranes in your nose are next to swell, and eventually you can't breath through your nostrils. Before it's over you begin to feel like you aren't too far from suffocating to death as you can tell your tongue is swelling too and will eventually close off your throat. This could go on for twenty-four hours at a time. In this hut, they could also almost cook you to death with large heaters on the walls. And, by blowing in outside air in the winter time they could freeze you to death in this stone hut."

The marine was remembering this in a very somber manner. He had spent time in there more than once! It was stuff like this that you heard about, that instilled a fear and anxiety in you that you absolutely couldn't and wouldn't think about while you were up there on that front line.

The NCO giving the briefing got to the Big Dipper in the sky. He pointed to a picture of it on an easel, and seriously said, "This Big Dipper is very important to you, and you better be able to find it in the heavens at night." He went on and told us how the outer two stars of the dipper cup are pointer stars. A straight line through them will point north and south. The upper star of the cup points north to the North Star, and the lower star of the cup points south. He went on telling us that if we were separated from our unit or escaping from capture, you should travel south only at night. Lay low and out of sight during the day. If captured, it was your duty to try and escape at all times. Well, I got so I could find that Big Dipper in a couple of seconds. I looked at it many a night. At that briefing, the NCO also handed out a little folded copy of the Twenty-third Psalm from the Old Testament. The Psalm that starts, "The Lord is my Shepherd," and ends, "I will dwell in the house of the Lord forever."

On the very first patrol we went out on, I found out I was not only a rifleman, but an ammunition bearer as well. The new man gets the lousy jobs. We were always pretty much loaded down on these patrols. Besides the cartridge clips all around your waist, there was a canteen full of water on one hip and a bayonet on the other hip. We always carried two bandoleers of cartridge clips crisscrossed over our chests and usually four hand grenades clipped to our shoulder straps. The shovel attached to your pack. The steel helmet on your head and the combat boots on your feet acted as counterbalances. The M1 rifle you carried weighed nine pounds. As we were forming up for the patrol, my squad leader came up to me and handed me two boxes of machine gun ammunition. They were attached, one on each end, to a webbed belt. This gave me eighteen more pounds to carry. I didn't realize it, but other guys had heavy loads too. A guy carrying a Browning Automatic Rifle (BAR) had a forty-pound load with his gun and ammo. Mortar bases were heavy as hell too.

Fox Company crossed over the front line and went out into the hilly terrain. About a half-mile out, we started to climb this hill. It wasn't too high a hill, but it was steep. We trudged straight up to the top without stopping. Being green as grass, I didn't know just when we were to start killing the enemy. I'm sure I was pale as a ghost and anxious looking as I put down the two boxes of ammo. One of the guys around me, pointed at me and loudly said, "Hey look at him. He didn't even break a sweat coming up this hill." We stayed right where we were for a couple of hours and then retraced our path back to our line. I was glad!

We would get our mail pretty regularly during this time. Marlene was writing to me every day! Oh, no! She was a nice girl so it just wasn't right to let her keep doing this. I just couldn't have her waiting for me to come home. I just couldn't plan anything at this time. I didn't really intend to write her a "Dear John" letter, but I guess that's the way she took it. I wrote and said she shouldn't really be writing every day and that I didn't know what I would be doing when I got home. I never heard from her again. That was sad!

It was three days later when we went on our second patrol. I was given my two boxes of machine gun ammo and two platoons of Fox Company, with a machine gun attachment, crossed the line again. The weather was fine, but the assignment wasn't that good. Our company lieutenant led us around all day. He had been briefed on our itinerary and destination. He knew the terrain and hill heights. We nosed our way up this valley and over into that valley. I don't know what he saw, but we hurriedly set up two different skirmish lines that day. I had to find the machine gun crew and bring them their ammo. I just stayed with them, lying in the grass. It was a welcome rest. Especially since the Chinese didn't want to fight that day.

It was about five o'clock in the afternoon when we gathered at the base of this hill and were told to take it easy. We were three and a half miles north of our line. We hadn't been there long when here comes our company Jeep. Our company Jeep driver and one guy from the mess tent was bringing us three big kettles of hot food. Boy, this was great, but it made you wonder what the hell was going on. We had a tray of good stuff that went down pretty fast. Then I spied the gallon can of jelly and loaves of bread. They had brought bread and jelly! I had to have some of that. About this time, the lieutenant and the platoon leaders and some of the guys started, one by one, to climb this hill behind us. There were four chowhounds still behind me as I picked up my two boxes of ammo and started up the hill. I took about ten steps and realized I was completely out of gas. My legs were like rubber and didn't want to go up this hill. I was resting as the last four guys passed me by. I took ten more steps and stopped and noticed the guys ahead of me were resting too. I heard the engine of the Jeep start up and watched them disappear around the bend. They were getting the hell out of here before the Chinese got zeroed in on 'em.

I was climbing the hill ten steps at a time. I looked up and fifty feet above me stood the lieutenant. Officers are trained to check the rear of their command if possible and that was what he was doing. Officers were pretty careful though, about getting too friendly with their men. This was so they wouldn't hesitate sending them out into harm's way. I'm sure he was equally interested in me and the machine gun ammunition. He wanted us both at the top of the hill. I took ten steps and the lieutenant would take ten steps, over and over. We were coming up a finger of the hill that several foxholes overlooked, so some of the guys were watching. My pup tent buddy, Bob Reusnow, had been made third platoon runner, so was with the third platoon CP, and was watching me struggle up the hill. I could just hear him say to the platoon sergeant, "A guy that has to carry his nuts around in a sack shouldn't have to be an ammo bearer." I finally got the ammo up to the machine gun emplacement. Wouldn't you know it was on the highest peak of the hill!

Jesus! What were we doing out here three and a half miles in front of the line? We were on a three-day outpost. I was buddied up with a guy named Tiny in a hole just below the machine gun emplacement. Tiny was a large fellow and a nice guy and had a little more experience at this than I did. I think, way down deep, I felt a small degree of safety with this big guy.

Night set in like someone had put a lid on a kettle. It was dark. We both just leaned against the backside of our hole, putting in time. Out of the blackness came the voices of Chinese soldiers. They were at the bottom of our hill. They sounded like they were close to where we had eaten our chow. Maybe four or five of 'em, the way the sounds were different. They jibber-jabbered, and then one hollered out and got a one word answer from some distance away. Then all fell quiet. Tiny, in a low voice, said to me, "Maybe they don't know we are up here." Then, more to himself rather than to me, he worried, "I hope Jensen keeps that trigger finger of his under control!" No one made a sound. It had been quiet for some time now, and pushing midnight, so Tiny suggested, "You take the first watch for about an hour and I'll try to get a few winks and then I'll take over." Tiny folded himself up into the corner of our hole as I started peering out into the darkness. God, it was black. You couldn't see a tree six feet in front of you. When those Chinese voices came up the hill I began to feel scared, cold, and dangerously tired. I could feel my whole body shake and was wondering if I could pull the trigger if I had to. I leaned forward on my elbows now with my rifle resting on the dirt from the hole. I couldn't see at all, so I did as much listening as looking. Was a Chinaman going to spray me with his burp gun or stick a bayonet in my throat?

I looked and listened, and looked, and looked, until my head gradually lowered itself onto my arm and I was fast asleep. Tiny must have awakened and took over. About 4:30 am we were jarred completely awake as the rain came down with a purpose. We had to get our ponchos out of our packs and get them on before we got soaked. That's why it was so dark. We were socked in with heavy dark clouds that blocked all light from the heavens. In another half hour some morning light did manage to penetrate through. We hadn't been attacked by Chinese and didn't even talk about it. We both opened a small can of corned beef hash out of our C rations. The Jeep driver had given all of us three days of C rations. The rain kept coming down.

It rained all day and was still coming down as we went into our second night on the outpost. No Chinese showed up. Not even to talk. That next day we were ordered to rig up some kind of cover over our holes, as the lieutenant thought by now they knew we were here and expected some artillery to come in. So, in the rain, Tiny and I cut some three-inch pine with our bayonets, and got a makeshift lean-to over us. It was still raining as we went through our third night. No Chinese and no artillery. The rain was stopping as the fourth morning of this patrol dragged on. We were told we were leaving the hill and going back to the line. Looking down on that finger, I couldn't climb, the first of the guys were leaving. There were two guys rocking back and forth on makeshift litters. That seemed really strange. The word was that their feet had shriveled up so bad from being wet for three nights and two days that they couldn't walk. I didn't carry the machine gun ammo off the hill. Someone else did. Little did I know though, my new job was going to be taking a turn at being lead scout.

We averaged over two patrols a week. When two companies went out, it seemed like Fox Company did a lot of this stuff with George Company. On one patrol on a moonlit night, we were walking in this trench on a finger of a hill. The guy in front of me turns and says, "We're walking on skeletons." I in turn, told the guy behind me, "We're walking on skeletons." The skulls and rib cages and long bones of a lot of men reflected the moonlight. Maybe they got caught in a napalm dropping.

When we had to go up on line for a few days during this patrol period, we sat by our bunkers that first day and watched Corsairs drop napalm across the valley from us. Two planes from aircraft carriers came down and dropped two 500-pound canisters each. They came in real low to make sure they hit the entrenched enemy. A huge ball of jellied gasoline spread out, engulfing the area. Two Corsairs came back the next day and did the same thing again. What a hideous way to die if you were on the receiving end of that stuff. Around midnight that night, I was pulling my hour on guard. Sitting outside our bunker and looking up north, there was this light coming out of the darkness of the sky. It kept getting bigger and bigger and then the sound of an airplane joined the light.

The outline of a four-engine bomber was soon visible. The inboard engine on the right side was on fire, illuminating the whole aircraft. It was a huge B-29 that was evidently hit up north while on a bombing mission. Not being able to make it back to their base in Japan, they were coming down south over land. With no place to land in Korea they knew they had to crash their plane, but didn't want to do it behind our lines. The pilots could tell when they had crossed our line because of a few scattered lights in the rear. They turned the big bird in a big circle and during this time I think everyone but the pilot bailed out into our rear area. He then flew the B-29 back across the line into enemy territory and bailed out himself. The plane circled by itself and then crashed into a hillside a couple of miles from me. Later the next day, the word was passed from bunker to bunker that the pilot of that plane was shot as he was making his way up to our line. Lots of things went on during those few days in a line bunker. It's really lousy when you get hurt or killed by your own people!

On another night patrol, our leaders, for some reason, decided to spend the night on the side of this hill. It had to be the hottest night of the summer with the humidity like ninety-nine percent. I hadn't noticed the mosquitoes until we lay down to get some rest. Man, they were thick. They could probably smell our dirty stinking bodies from all over Korea. We were forced to curl up in a fetal position under our ponchos and make it airtight.

You could hear them humming and buzzing trying to get in. Now, it was like a sauna, and the sweat saturated your fatigues. Morning came and back to our patrol base we went. That really was the only time that mosquitoes were a problem. We did have mosquito netting for our pup tent at our patrol base. Funny, all the time I was in Korea and living like an animal, there were no animals to be seen. No dogs or cats, no birds or rabbits, not even a snake! I'm sure that the hungry armies and civilians had eaten most of them.

Some Chinese infiltrators had been causing some trouble behind our lines, so we went on a long day patrol behind our lines trying to find a trace of them. It was probably the Han River that we followed downstream for a half day and crossed over it on a pontoon bridge that the army engineers had built. Then we went upriver on the other side, back toward our patrol base. We poked around in the underbrush in places an infiltrator might hide, but found no signs of anyone.

In the late afternoon, the lieutenant began to look for a place where we could wade back across the river. This is something we had to do. The damn river was full. From bank to bank there was a lot of water going down from heavy rains. At this wide place, where it was more calm, he asked for a volunteer to go on out and see how deep it got. No problem getting a volunteer. In he went. It just kept getting deeper and deeper. With his rifle over his head he was out in the middle. The water was up to his neck. He did manage to keep on going and made it across to the other side. This crossing was going to be over the head of a lot of short guys, so upriver we went. The next try was at some pretty vicious looking rapids. With the lieutenant leading the way, we entered one by one. Our feet began feeling for solid footing as our bodies headed into the rushing water. The pressure against your knees made each step treacherous. My group was out in the middle when a guy several men in front of me lost his footing, fell in, and started helplessly and dangerously tumbling from rock to rock downstream. In a split second, not one but two guys, without even thinking of themselves, high hurtled after this poor guy washing down river. They both unslung their rifles on the way and let them drop in the river. Managing to stay on their own feet, they reached the guy simultaneously and pulled him to his feet. Then hand in hand they slowly came up together and joined our single file again. God, those two rescuers were brave! In that rushing water, you had all you could handle just taking care of yourself. Getting to your feet after you'd been knocked down was almost impossible. Deep water again was just downriver from the rapids. This crossing of the river must have been terrifying to a guy who couldn't swim. And with all the weight we carried, you could go to the bottom in a hurry, like a deep-sea diver. I'm not a strong swimmer. I just couldn't be that brave. Could I? No! We made it back to our base. We lost three rifles and a helmet on that patrol.

George and Fox Companies were out again nosing around, asking for trouble four miles out. The frantic word was passed back from man to man, "Dig in, there's a Chinese regiment on the other side of the hill!" We were all shocked into action. Grabbing that little shovel off our packs, none of us looked up or stopped digging until our holes began to look like they were one and a half feet deep and four and a half feet long. Those holes were dug in record-breaking time! We were sweating as we sat on the edge of our holes, watching, waiting, and listening. In about a half hour's time, the word was passed, "We're moving out. Going back the same way we came." On back to base camp we went. The next day my shoulders, arms, and back were really sore from digging non-stop all tensed up. I guess that's why there were so many holes on the tops of the hills in Korea.

Fox Company went out again. I was informed I was the lead scout on this patrol. I was now a lead scout along with Frank Bailey. Frank was from the third platoon, just like I was. He was a husky, likable fellow. He and I would be alternating on the upcoming patrols. We were both up front with the lieutenant, the first sergeant, the first platoon sergeant and his corporal platoon runner, and a forward observer from B Battery of our field artillery battalion, as we passed through the line and headed north. The forward observer carried a real good radio for contacting the 105-mm Howitzers in his outfit.

Being a lead scout can be something like being out on an outpost. When called upon you could be sticking your neck out, usually all by yourself. We had covered a lot of ground; the lieutenant always in front. I'm still not any good at spotting Chinese soldiers in the bush. It's not like spotting Chinese pheasants in the tumbleweeds of Nebraska. Maybe the lieutenant saw a Chink; I don't know, but I was called forward. "I want you to go down into this ravine and up to the top of the other side and take a good look around." The lieutenant was alternately pointing and looking at me. "Then come on back." The top of the other side was about forty yards away. So, down I went, slow and deliberate, sweeping my head from side to side. I didn't like doing this. Looking down, when I reached the top of the other side, I saw a single set of brand new fresh tennis shoe tracks made in the soft ground. The tracks may have been made by the Chink the lieutenant saw. There was no one in sight though and nothing else to be seen from where I stood. I didn't venture right or left. It wouldn't be possible to follow the tennis shoe tracks as they quickly disappeared in ground cover. I didn't feel that brave anyway. I turned around and came back. I told the lieutenant what I had seen. He didn't say anything in return. In a few minutes he did say, "We're going home." Back to the line we went. Frank Bailey and I took turns being lead scout on the next several patrols. Neither he nor I was called upon to do any scouting.

We didn't have a forward observer for artillery along with us too often, but on this day we did. It was a two-company patrol with Fox Company out front. We had an extra lieutenant from the other company up front with us. It was Frank's turn to be lead scout. Our lieutenant was leading the way. He always had his field glasses and used them a lot. Nosing around, looking for trouble, he spotted some Chinese on the crest of the hill in front of us. They were probably on patrol just like we were. They were quickly out of sight.

We all moved about fifty yards toward the hill. The lieutenant called Frank forward and told him to slowly go out another twenty-five yards, taking cover as he went. Constantly checking the hilltop with his field glasses, the lieutenant again spotted some heads sticking up. He decided to bring in some artillery to bear on our enemy's hill. He and the forward observer were on the radio giving coordinates to the rear 105s. The lieutenant whistled and motioned for Frank to come back with us.

Frank came back, but stopped still a part way out. Frank knew we had called for artillery. I could hear the forward observer loudly say into the radio, "Fire for range and distance." The first round came roaring in. It blasted the upper hillside with perfect distance. With a fraction of a degree left the next round would be right on top of where the Chinks were. They quickly called for that second round. We had all dispersed a little and were hugging the ground as this was going on. I was lying right beside the lieutenant from the other company. The second round was angrily roaring way too loud, way too close. It made you grab your steel helmet with both hands and hold on. They must have traversed right instead of left, and threw that shell in just above where Frank was laying.

The blast was frightening. I don't remember what I heard first. The lieutenant on the radio or the frantic call for, "Medic, medic!" The lieutenant was screaming into the radio, "Get that goddamn stuff off of us. Cease fire, cease fire!" "Medic, medic," the guys that had gone up by Frank were calling. Two medics ran by us in a couple of seconds. They must have headed toward the explosion as soon as they heard it. "Medic, Medic!" the lieutenant lying beside me hollered. It scared the shit out of me. I looked at him as he struggled to raise himself on his elbows. "My leg, my leg. I'm hit in the leg!" he was saying through the pain. I sat up and looked at his legs. I couldn't see where he was hit. There wasn't any tear in his fatigues or blood anywhere. I didn't know what to do. The fact that he was a lieutenant seemed to make it harder to lean over and put my hands on him.

My lieutenant solved my problem when he screamed, "We are moving out!" All of us but the two guys that were hit were on our feet and moving out. The lieutenant that had lain beside me hollered for a medic again as I was leaving him. I'm sure he got attention in a bit. I think our lieutenant was really mad and was going up to settle with them Chinks on the hill. We all had to walk past where Frank was laying. I think Frank was hurt bad. The two medics were huddled around him, making it hard to even see him. As I passed directly over him, I found it hard to look down.

We kind of stormed straight up to the hilltop where the Chinese had been seen. There was no one there. The lieutenant looked and looked with his field glasses. He finally said, "We're gonna head back." The two wounded guys were gone when we reached the area where the artillery had come in. Back at camp the word was passed that Frank had died. Shrapnel had torn his leg loose at the groin and he had bled to death before they could get him off the hill. Shrapnel is ugly stuff that can range from as small as a needle to the size of a small dishpan and can be unbelievably sharp and jagged. The big pieces can literally cut you in two.

At the Korean War Memorial in Washington, D.C. they have a couple of computers that contain the names of all the guys who were killed in Korea. In the fall of 1998, when we were visiting D.C., I typed Frank's name into the computer several different ways. The computer would not confirm that Frank had been killed. Again, in Korea, the word passed by us guys from one to the other was often just a half-truth or a rumor. We weren't told and had no way of knowing the real truth. Even official accounts of events are reported differently by people who were there. And these accounts are written up by people who weren't there using the information they were told.

Don Sell, Keith Sloan, Lloyd Foust, Frank Bailey,
Ted Eveling. (L-R)
All in the third platoon. Frank didn't make it.

HILL 717, OUR LAST OUTPOST

For two months now, we had been patrolling pretty steadily. It was Sunday, 2 September 1951, the day before Labor Day back home. We were sent out to do the worst thing yet. Fox Company was sent to an outpost seven and a half miles north of the front line. This outpost was on top of hill 717. Hills in Korea were designated or named by their height. Hill 717 is 717 meters above sea level. This was real no man's land and we were a long way from help. The 105mm Howitzers that backed us up could only fire a thirty-three-pound shell seven miles. We were out as far or beyond their ability to cover us.

Anyway, it was a nice day and our cautious trip was uneventful. Korea is a very beautiful country. It's one of the hilliest countries on earth. The Koreans had done some clever engineering when they terraced these hills for water flow and rice production.

After we had climbed to the top, I was assigned a foxhole to occupy all by myself. It was a hole that had already been dug. Maybe a Chinese guy dug it. This hole was at the top of the finger that the whole company had just climbed up, a finger the Chinese might use to come up! It was kind of obvious that this hill had been fought over before. We had three days of C rations in our packs. We ate another part of one that night on top of the hill. I had a small can of cold beans and wieners, round crackers, and an enriched chocolate candy bar plus water from my canteen. I don't remember much about sleep that night. I had no buddy, so an hour on and an hour off wasn't possible. It was quiet anyway.

The next morning, 3 September, was very cloudy and in a short time I could hear and then see rain coming up the valley. It was upon us in no time, heavy and on the cold side. So, there I sat under my poncho, along with my rifle, bandoleers of ammunition, hand grenades, pack, and shovel. The helmet was a natural crown for this configuration. It rained hard all day long. My hole was below me and full of six inches of water. Little did I know that maybe this rain had the Chinese holed up too and probably saved my life. The rain stopped in the early evening and the second night was spent staring down the slope of the finger and listening for something. I fell off to sleep every so often. The next morning, 4 September, the only thing sticking out of the low hanging clouds as far as I could see in any direction was hill 717. It was like having gone to heaven. Extremely impressive, peaceful, and beautiful! Korea is known as "The Land of the Morning Calm."

You could almost hear the water running out and down the hill from the rain. About fifteen yards down below me, there were a couple of springs gushing pure clean water. Me and the two guys in holes beside me filled our canteens. I hadn't really talked to them because the holes they were in were just about out of sight from me. The way we were spread out would really make a weak defense of the hilltop.

I hadn't seen my squad leader or anybody for directions or encouragement for two days!

We were told that third morning that Item Company was on its way out to relieve us. This was good news. About one o'clock that afternoon they started showing up and by two o'clock we were on our way back to the front lines, another cautious uneventful trip. It was nice that night to lay down in our pup tent with a sleeping bag and a roof over our heads. It's amazing how two bodies and a candle burning in a pup tent can warm it up to a cozy temperature. We spent the next day cleaning things up and getting some more good chow in our bellies.

Item Company was spending their second night on top of hill 717. Love Company had come out and joined Item that day, making two companies out there now. Maybe our intelligence system had observed some enemy activity so the power of command beefed up the outpost, and just in time! For two hours, between 9 pm and 11 pm, all hell broke loose as the Chinese started and sustained a massive artillery and mortar barrage directed at the top of hill 717. Communications to the companies and forward observers were lost. Following the bombardment, more than a regiment of Chinese stormed up the hill. Fighting in the dark is like a nightmare you never want to have. This reinforced regiment of Chinese, with over a thousand men, was coming up to kill and capture about 275 of our guys on the hill. By mid afternoon the next day they had control of the whole area.

There was just a hint of daylight when we got the frantic word in our pup tent and were told to double time it! We got breakfast and then hurriedly prepared to go out to hill 717. I don't know how many men were ahead of me as we made our way single file away from the front lines. Things were not like the march we had made previously. It was stop and go, as I'm sure the front of the column was getting some small arms and mortar fire from the Chinese.

About a mile out we were picking our way along this shear cliff with a canal full of water at its base. We all hit the rocky ground as we heard the mortar shells explode about fifty yards ahead of us. The word was passed back for everyone to get into the water of the canal, and everyone did in a hurry. A lot of guys went in with their rifles and got them wet. I left mine lying outside. There were no more mortar rounds, so we got out of the ditch and proceeded on. Fifty yards up, two guys stood bleeding. The shrapnel from the mortars that had been bounced off the shear rock cliff above had hit them. They both had a dozen places they were losing blood from, but they all seemed to be superficial wounds from small pieces of shrapnel. These two rounds that came in may have been of the antipersonnel kind. That's a shell designed to break into small pieces and wound a maximum number of soldiers rather than kill 'em. An NCO was encouraging these two guys to make their way back if they could. No medics around? We got word that out in front of us a medic was killed and another guy gravely injured by this incoming mortar.

We proceeded on in a stop and go manner. You could hear an ever-increasing amount of artillery going over our heads from our front lines. They had quickly ordered up a couple of batteries of 155mm Howitzers. They could lob a 95-pound shell 9.3 miles. You could see these big projectiles as they roared through the sky!

It was about this time that a strong pungent odor of pine started to permeate the air. It was a bad smell! Artillery from both sides was chewing up the pine trees into little pieces. We slowly continued on. Around mid afternoon, we were on the side of this hill, held up, and not going anywhere. This lieutenant comes up to me and says, "Give me a drink of water." A deep scowl entered my face as we looked into each other's eyes. As I hesitated, I was saying to myself, "Drink your own water you son of a bitch. Who in the hell are you anyway?" He wasn't going away. He hadn't said, "That's an order soldier!" I didn't take my eyes off his as I slowly unsnapped my canteen and handed it to him. Watching him like a hawk, he took a small swallow and was gone. He didn't even say thanks. He must have been an officer from George Company.

I thought back to basic training, when we walked fourteen miles and then were asked to do a map reading exercise. Most of us couldn't walk any further, so watched as a few went the extra mile. Maybe this lieutenant was working his ass off trying to get us out of this mess and needed that swallow of water? By nightfall that first day, we had got about one third of the way out to hill 717. We were on top of this smaller hill and were told to dig in. I was at the base of this tree and digging was next to impossible. I quietly worked on my hole all night, not sleeping a wink. I was excited and scared and thankful that I hadn't been in my hole on top of hill 717 the night before looking down that finger the Chinese were coming up!

The next morning we were up and on the move. We hadn't been given any C rations as we hurriedly left the front lines, so we didn't have anything to eat. We moved out single file again and it was slow going. The front of our column had to be sure they weren't taking us into an ambush. At one spot that morning, looking down at the path we were following, there laid a part of a human torso, a reminder of what was going on. The smell of pine wouldn't let you forget either. The North Koreans and the Chinese, if at all possible, would bury their dead or take them with 'em. This way their enemy would not know of their successes. Things were quiet as we made our way, staying on the sides of hills.

Around mid afternoon, a single mortar round came in close to us. It seemed to thud into the ground about thirty-five feet from us and didn't go off. It was a dud. Mortar rounds come straight down. You can't hear them until they have almost hit the ground, so you don't have much time to hit the ground yourself. The mortar round coming in told us they were still around and made you wonder how many and how strong.

By evening of this second day we were pretty much at the base of hill 717. For the night, it was decided that George Company would form a perimeter around the top of this small hill we were on and Fox Company would gather in the middle. That was a break for us because we didn't have to stand guard. Not having slept the night before, I was dead tired.

In the middle of the night, George Company had a short firefight that barely woke me. I don't know if they were shooting at something or if there were nervous trigger fingers. No one was shaking us awake in the morning telling us to get ready to go up hill 717. The sun was above the horizon as I woke up and lay there with the rest of the guys. Thirsty as hell, I decided I would finish the last swallow in my canteen. I had been saving it. When I tipped my head and canteen back, nothing came out. Someone had drunk my last swallow while I was sleeping. It seemed like my canteen of water was not only important to me, but to two other guys as well!

Back in July, about two weeks after I joined Fox Company, we had a young lad in our platoon shoot himself in the foot to escape this predicament he could no longer handle. He was with the company before I got there, so may have been in on some of that bloody fighting, and maybe even hand-to-hand combat that took place in March through June. He just couldn't take it anymore. He was a regular enlistee and the way he looked he may have only been seventeen years old. His foot wound only took six weeks to heal, so he had just returned to the company before we went out to hill 717. To shoot yourself, you have to be mentally and physically unable to cope anymore. You can feel fear and anxiety like you've never known. It happens and it's nothing to be ashamed of. Tough career marines have been known to freeze in combat right where they laid or stood, unable to move or fire their weapons with their guns still on safety. I'm not sure I agree with the army's policy of sending shell-shocked kids back into combat.

So, on this third morning, 9 September, we were ready to go back up hill 717. We hadn't eaten for two days and all of us were parched from thirst. There hadn't been a stream anywhere we could have got some water in our canteens. I guess we were hugging the hillsides too much. Single file, we pushed off and headed up hill. Heavy artillery fire had stopped in the late afternoon of the first day, so things had been pretty quiet in that respect. I didn't think much about what or whom we would find on top of the hill. Attacking in the daytime helped a hell of a lot. To do this at night would be unimaginable. Word was passed back not to fire our weapons because they didn't want them to know where we were. We were in pretty thick scrub pines. Only a few minutes after that word was passed back, someone down below me fired his rifle. And it was just a minute after that that the young lad that had shot himself in the foot went out of his head. He, too, was just below me and was a real mess. He was burying his face in the dirt and alternately crying and yelling, "Don't let them get me. Don't let them get me!" It was impossible to get him to his feet or talk to him.

Our platoon sergeant told Bill Secrist and I and two other guys to make a litter out of a poncho and carry him back. Carrying him back seemed like a large order. We weren't sure how to get back. We could kind of see the area where we had spent last night and jumped off from about forty-five minutes ago. We decided to head that way in a straight line.

We left the column carrying this guy on a poncho. Doing this kind of tore you this way and that. We were leaving the safety of being with the rest of the companies. Us five guys were now out here in the boonies all by ourselves, but it didn't seem like we would have to be attacking hill 717. The young kid wasn't quiet and was tough to handle. The third time we stopped and earnestly told him that we were headed back to the front line, and that everything was going to be all right, he finally calmed down and we got him to his feet. That was a real break, but thinking about going back and finding our company was out of the question.

We kept heading in a southerly direction. We reached the exact place where we had spent last night. We were shocked as we walked up to two dead guys lying on the ground. They were Chinese. They were stripped naked with their little peters sticking straight up in the air. South Korean laborers that carried supplies for us would totally strip the dead because they needed the clothes and shoes. I guess we were too far away to hear any shooting. We sure wondered who in the world shot these two guys and stripped 'em. Bullet holes weren't really obvious in front and we weren't about to turn them over and look. We were looking at these two guys, and looking for the best way to head out next, when we heard the whine of a Jeep engine. Way off in the trees, we could see movement of men. We were sure they were our guys, so happily headed their way. We joined this new column of men headed north; only us five guys kept going south, back to the main line.

Our guys from the third platoon went on up hill 717 with the rest of the troops without encountering any Chinese. They said, while milling around up there, they were strafed by one of our carrier based navy Corsairs. A .50-caliber bullet passed through the wrist of a guy from our platoon and his hand fell to the ground. He wore horn-rimmed glasses. I don't remember his name. They had put down their identification panels so aircraft could see we were friendly troops, but the pilot evidently didn't see them or saw them too late. We hadn't seen an airplane all week. Then this one had to come along.

So, the guys told us that there was no one up there on hill 717. There was not a trace of the men from Item and Love Companies. Again, the talk amongst us was grim and everyone thought undoubtedly that all of them had been killed, captured, or carted off. Everyone thought we were really lucky that Fox Company wasn't up there all by ourselves that night.

The fact was that Item and Love Companies fought hard as they withdrew, letting the Chinese have the hills. Approximately two-thirds of the two companies were either killed in action, wounded, or missing. People who were involved first hand with Item and Love Companies have reported this. I had been with Fox Company ten weeks when this event happened.

I have written to a disabled Korean vet living in an old house in Greenwich, Ohio with other veterans. He told me about the book *Official History of the 25th Infantry Division in Korea*. It covers the first year and a half of the three-year war. In the book they use a page to describe the hill 717 incident. They talk about the seriousness of the event, but talk a lot about the support that was brought up to help in the situation. They say we went out and recaptured hill 717 in one day when it took three days, and they never mention the lost men. I thought I would write it down as it was with us.

My fellow litter bearer, Bill Secrist, from Chicago. He had done some professional dancing. He's sitting on his helmet to stay off the cold ground. Note his mittens on a string. Precious, can't lose them in battle. Taken in reserve area.

If we were lucky, we might get a warm shower here with river water.

Mills and Evans. Would have made a good comedy team. Evans, on the right, was one of our great Fox Company Jeep drivers.

RESERVE FOR AWHILE AND BACK UP ON THE LINE

After ten weeks of patrols and the disaster on hill 717, the Second Battalion was ready for a rest. Item and Love Companies had to be rebuilt! Our Fox Company lieutenant, who had led us on all those patrols, was promoted to captain. He had done an especially good job the week of hill 717. He would probably go back to battalion now and serve in some capacity back there.

Reserve area was a peaceful place to be. We were housed in large squad tents with a drip oil stove. We were still sleeping on the ground, but eating well. Only a couple of days went by before we were climbing up one of those damn hills every morning after breakfast. We would go up and work on a blocking line. They were building lines to fall back to in case the hoards of Chinese drove us back off the 38th parallel again. I think there was a Kansas line and a Wyoming line. We would work all day on bunkers. We would cut and use the largest timber we could find. We also went to a mountainous section of this backup line. For three days, we strung barbwire in steep, almost impossible places. You needed to be a mountain goat. It seemed kind of dumb to string wire there, but maybe the Chinese could find a good place like that to get through. We were on C rations, and working your ass off made you more hungry than C rations could take care of. I went around a couple of those evenings asking the guys, "You going to eat your enriched chocolate candy bar?" Some of the guys didn't like them, so it was easy to get some extra bars.

In fourteen days, our so-called resting time was over. With a new commander we went back up to the main line and into bunkers that other companies were vacating. This was my first semi-permanent bunker home. I was paired up with Don Sell. He was a good looking, pretty strong kid from Los Angeles. Don always had grin on his face and didn't take things too seriously. He had inherited one of them heavy Browning Automatic Rifles to carry around. From this point on, all night long, it was sleep an hour and guard an hour. This was the standing order on the front line. It was called the buddy system. We all had wristwatches, so we would know when our hour of guard was up. We'd wake our buddy up and he'd get out of his sleeping bag and you would crawl into yours for a one-hour sleep. I guess we could average five hours of sleep a night this way if it weren't for the rats. Rats! Huge suckers. I caught a glimpse of one once in the daylight. Otherwise, they were out and about mostly at night. The one I saw was over a foot long, with a seven-inch body and a seven-inch tail.

There was a toe of a tennis shoe sticking out of the ground about six feet above our bunker. I had noticed it several times those first few days we were there. I decided to stick something into it. I picked up a small stick and poked the sharp end of it into the top of the toe and then pulled it back out. Through the hole that I made came this thick gray matter oozing out. "My God!" I muttered half out loud. "There's a body buried here. Looks like they covered him up right where he laid dead. How many more dead soldiers are buried around here? That's what the rats are eating!" That's what made sleeping in our bunker a nightmare. The rats had honeycombed the roof of our bunker and would knock dirt down on your face as you tried to get your hour of sleep. You worried a rat would jump down on your face and start eating your eyeballs out. You could just hear them saying to themselves, "Ah, here's a fresh one." Don and I didn't talk about it much. We didn't even bother to cover up the tennis shoe.

Don fell asleep on guard a couple of times. Hell, we were tired. He tried to cover up by saying, "I decided to pull two hours of guard, so you can guard for two hours." Heck, we both knew what had happened. Bob Reusnow, our third platoon runner and my pup tent buddy, would drop by with bits of information now and then. I mentioned to Bob that Don had fallen asleep on guard. On the way back to the third platoon CP, Bob told our squad leader about Don falling asleep. So, here comes our squad leader, "You guys can't be doing this. Chinks sneak up on guys all the time and throw grenades in their holes. You can't be doing it!" And then he left. I didn't mean for Don to get in trouble. I remember when I fell asleep on guard! We both managed to do our hour on and hour off after that. And maybe that was a good thing. There was Chink trouble out in front of us.

You'd be sitting there on guard and there would be this small burst of fire in the air and a parachute flare would light up the sky and slowly drift to the ground. The light from these things was an eerie white, and it would swing back and forth a little on its parachute, which seemed to give movement to things. The shadows of tree trunks would also move as the flare got closer and closer to the ground.

These flares weren't called for for the fun of it. Someone sensed something going on, or maybe even a patrol called for them. There for a while, we'd get flares two or three times a week.

One day Don and I were sitting outside our bunker when we heard this big boom down in the valley to our right. A tank had just blown up in a big ball of flame. We were about a half-mile from this thing going up, but had a good vantage point for watching. We could see there were men all around this burning tank and a second tank was out there with them. About the time we had figured this much out, BOOM goes the second tank in another big ball of fire. They had run over some large land mines and the way they blew up and were burning, it didn't seem like anyone would be able to get out of them.

We had been told that this hill out in front of the valley was honeycombed with Chinese and that sniper fire and other activity from there was an ongoing problem. Don and I were a good ways up and back from that hill, putting us out of range of their rifle fire. The men that were being supported by the tanks continued working their way out toward the enemy's hill. We couldn't hear any rifle fire from where we were, but it seemed like they got pinned down and had to eventually give up and work their way back to the line. We heard that the men were from the platoons of George Company, which was on our right flank. There was no word on the guys in the tanks. The land mines that the tanks triggered had been set some dark night by the Chinese. How long they had been there no one knew. The mines were maybe seventy-five yards out from the bunkers guarding the trough of the valley, right under our noses. It didn't seem like you could get your mind off what happened down there with those tanks burning all day long and the tank crews probably still inside. The tanks would have been fully loaded with ammunition that would burn and explode, along with many gallons of diesel fuel and oil in the engine.

With this scary stuff going on, the practice seemed to spread across the line. We all started setting trip grenades out in front of our bunkers at night. In the morning we would go down and bring them up. It was rocky and pretty steep out in front of our bunker, which made it pretty hard for any Chinks to walk right up and get us. Don and I would take turns putting out two trip grenades. We would anchor the grenade with large rocks, so it was firmly held in place, but still giving the handle the ability to fly off when the pin was pulled. We'd then string communication wire from an anchor, like a tree trunk, over to the grenade. Communication wire was lying around all over the hills. We'd then almost straighten the pin on the grenade and tie the wire to the pull ring. Then we'd carefully crawl up to our bunker making sure we didn't dislodge a rock big enough to roll down, trip the wire, and blow ourselves up. It was really an accident waiting to happen. We all did something like this for about a week. The lieutenant put a stop to it when he found out what we were doing.

One morning I was told I was due, and had to go down the hill and get a tetanus booster. We had to walk down to where trucks were waiting for us. They hauled us to a first aid station that was further back. It took time for the guys to come from all parts of the line and fill the trucks. We were fed a noontime meal when we got to the first aid area and then started to get our shots in the first aid tent. I must have been eating jelly bread again because I was one of the last guys to go into the tent.

We had to stack our rifles in a rack before going into the tent. When I came out there were only three rifles on the rack, none of them mine. The last two guys quickly grabbed two of them leaving me with this old beat up gun that hardly had any bluing left on it. The last truck driver was standing by his open door and hollering at me, "Come on, let's go!" I grabbed the rifle, took one step, and down I went to my knees. The blood left my head and I was ready to keel over. The first aid people rushed out and helped me over to a tree stump. They told me to keep my head down a little and sit there for a minute. At the end of the minute I got up, took one step, and down I went again. The truck driver hollered again, "I've got to get these guys up to the line before dark. I've got to go!" The medics hollered back, "Give him one more minute and he'll be all right." In one more minute I was all right. I got on the truck with my old rifle and back to my rat-infested graveyard home I went. I had had dozens of shots before and none of them had ever made me woozy. The tetanus serum and the jelly must not have gotten along.

I was still mad about my rifle. "I don't even know if this damn thing works," I muttered. I had to know, because my life could depend on it. My squad leader got the third platoon sergeant on the sound powered phone and told him I'd like to fire a few rounds through it to see if it worked. The sergeant said to fire a clip through it. I don't know where we got some tracer rounds, but I reloaded a clip and put in three tracer cartridges with the other five, and fired 'em up north toward the Chinese. The tracer rounds left a red path that fell to the ground much like a rainbow. The old rifle, which had evidently covered many miles, worked fine.

Several weeks went by. It seemed to be pretty quiet all around us. My fairy godmother was at work. I was called over to the platoon CP. The platoon sergeant threw a question out to me, "How would you like to be third platoon company runner?" I looked at my pup tent buddy Bob. He was grinning and nodding his head up and down encouraging me to say yes. It was easy to tell Bob had suggested me for the job. The sergeant went on to say, "As company runner you would be staying at the Fox Company CP where the company lieutenant and first sergeant are. You would be under the communications sergeant along with runners from the other three platoons. You would be watching out for us guys in the third platoon. You'll be maintaining the phone lines of the third platoon as a wireman and be worked into being a radio operator. It's a good job and I'd like to see you take it." I looked at Bob again and wondered why in the world he wasn't taking it? He was still nodding his head. So I said, "Yeah, I'd like to be our company runner." The reason for the opening was our present third platoon company runner was rotating home. This was a nice break for me. First off, I'd be leaving the rat-infested graveyard bunker to poor Don. He'd be getting a new buddy. Secondly, I'd be in a bunker on the south side of the hills. All four platoon CPs and the company CPs were on the south side of the hills. They were out of direct sight of the enemy and possible snipers and in the wintertime you would not be staring directly into the face of the freezing wind sweeping down through Korea from Siberia.

The main part of my new job was to help watch our company switchboard twenty-four hours a day. I moved into a large bunker with the communications sergeant and the three runners. The lieutenant and first sergeant were in a nearby bunker. We had a small switchboard, but it weighed forty pounds and was bigger than a breadbox. It had six drops coming from six input lines. An incoming ringing current would energize a small solenoid, releasing a drop. We would have to see or hear this drop, answer the guy calling in, and patch and ring him to whomever he wanted to talk to. The most important line was back to battalion, where our lieutenant would get daily briefings. The lieutenant's phone took up a line and the other four lines went out to the four platoon CPs. So night and day, us five guys had to have someone sitting at the switchboard. A couple hours each night and maybe three or four hours in the daytime would cover this. This was sure better than an hour on and an hour off out on the line and there were no rats here.

Just a few days had gone by when here came my pup tent buddy Bob. He was at the company CP to get a SCR 300 field radio that weighed forty pounds, as the third platoon was sending out a ten-man night patrol and he was going to be the radio operator. This made me real nervous because I was supposed to be working into being a radio operator and anything the third platoon did could involve me. At that point in time I hadn't had any instructions on our radios. Leo Wright, the commo sergeant, showed Bob and I how to operate this 300 radio. There wasn't that much to it. There was a talk-listen button and a squelch potentiometer to turn for best signal to noise level. That was it. Bob was all excited about doing this. As I've said before, he was kind of enthusiastic about being in Korea. I have to admit I was glad Bob was going on that night patrol and not me. They went on their patrol and we listened for a call from them at the company CP. No call. Nothing happened.

I think SCR stood for Signal Corp Radio. Our SCR 300 and our SCR 536 walkie-talkie were World War II relics. They transmitted and received with a frequency modulation (FM) signal. That meant they operated best in a line of sight transmission. When you stick one of Korea's hilly hills between the transmitter and the receiver, the signal can't get through. We didn't have the occasion to really have to rely on them. I'm sure others did. Batteries for them were also a big problem.

A couple weeks before Christmas 1951, we had been on line for over two months and a replacement unit was on their way. It looked like we were going to be in reserve for Christmas! A shower and a change of clothes was going to be a great Christmas present! Don wasn't going to have to live with the rats anymore, but some other poor guys were.

My pup tent buddy Bob Reusnow and I, at the third platoon CP.
Note the wire cutters in my belt.

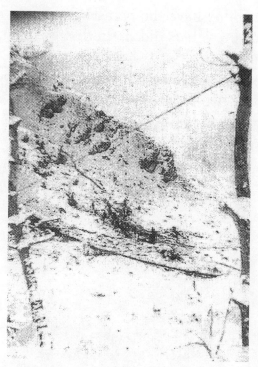

Chow area. The guys would leave their bunkers to get some warm food the laborers had brought up. We ate a lot of "C" rations otherwise.

Don Sell, with his Browning Automatic Rifle. Don was from Los Angeles. He was my buddy in that rat infested bunker.

Chigu, Kim and Lee. South Koreans. Radio carriers and interpreters for Fox Company.

CHRISTMAS 1951

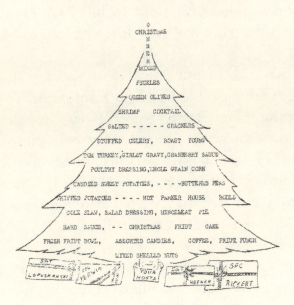

As you can see from the above original menu, we were very lucky and well taken care of. I'm sure most of the guys still up on line got some warm turkey and gravy too. The Korean laborers would get it up to them on their backs. Maybe they got a package from home too. But, they wouldn't have all these trimmings!

It was great. The people back home sure hadn't forgotten us. The government, friends, neighbors, and parents were all supporting what we had to do over here. I think they say it takes about ten people in the immediate rear to keep one soldier up on line. And every one of them, from the great mess workers to the medical staff in our Mobile Army Surgical Hospitals (MASH) were taking care of us with a lot of dedication and worry. Our Fox Company Jeep driver was a supporter too. He amazed me. Always on the go. Hauling someone or something here and there, tearing out into enemy territory to deliver some ammo or food or haul back someone wounded. He was driving his Jeep in that column of men and supplies going out to hill 717. He deserved a medal. Fox Company had two different Jeep drivers while I was there.

Christmas Eve in our squad tent was joyous. Most of the guys got one or more packages from home, so there was much sharing. "Hey, taste these cookies," someone would say. "Pass these brownies around, they're delicious!" another guy shared. Guys got little personal things too from their folks and lovers. I even got some shorts. It was a night of laughter and camaraderie. We all had our beer ration of two cans that loosened everyone up. But 3.2% alcohol in military beer doesn't loosen you up too much.

Six days later it was New Year's Eve. We had our weekly beer ration again, but we didn't exactly give a whistle blowing welcome to 1952. I wasn't looking forward to another year of this. In another few days it turned cold as hell. One night it was—27 degrees. I was glad we weren't in our holes up on the line.

Korean laborers coming up the hill with supplies, water, and food. They could really carry a load on their backs using "A" frames.

Outdoor kitchen for Korean labor gang. That's rice in the big bowl and some kind of fish stew in the steaming one.

BACK TO THE LINE

We did head back up to the line the first part of January. That reserve didn't last long. It had warmed up a lot though, so that helped. We had a new company commander again. Us five guys wound up in a pretty nice communications bunker. Usually, these company communications bunkers had a dirt shelf all around, about two feet high. Four guys could throw a sleeping bag on this shelf and get some sleep. The fifth guy was always on the switchboard. It was pretty crowded in most bunkers, but this one was one of the better ones. Leo Wright, our commo sergeant, had gone up with an advance party to find out where these bunkers were that we had to move into. We were replacing the company that had been there. We would hook up the phone lines to our switchboard that they had used. Amazing how these communication lines usually worked when we made these moves.

Bob called, though, from the third platoon and said he needed some wire for a bad sound-powered phone line to the bunker of the third squad leader. I grabbed a spool of wire and my wire cutters and headed for the third platoon. Bob pointed out where the bunker of the squad leader was.

Giving him his end of the wire, I started a new line. This was on the north side of the hill.

I couldn't believe the maze of wire that had been strung, mostly along the same route. If you gathered it all together you would have a three-inch cable with a hundred conductors. These lines had been severed many times because a lot of fighting was always taking place there. I had never worked in the target pits on the firing range back at basic training. If I had, I would have better learned what bullets zinging over your head sounded like. As I was laying this line I had to momentarily freeze a couple of times and say to myself, "What was that?" The hairs on my neck were saying, "Is someone shooting at me?" Man, I hustled to the bunker of the squad leader, dropped in, and hooked up my end of the wire to his sound-powered phone. I whistled into the phone and Bob picked up on the other end. It worked. Without saying much to the guys in the hole, I retraced my path on the run and headed back to the company CP.

Guys were routinely getting to go on R&R back to Tokyo. You had to have put about seven months in Korea to have your name come up. You got five days of rest and recuperation. Two of the five days were spent getting to Tokyo and back. You did spend four nights in Tokyo. (Not all of the R&R guys got to go to Tokyo.)

One of our company runners had left for his R&R a day before we left reserve to come up on line. He was back now and spending his second night with us in our new position on line. I was pulling the midnight to 2 am shift on the switchboard. The single candle that we burned dimly lit the dirt-walled bunker. This guy that had just returned from R&R began to sob. He was close enough for me to reach out and touch him. When he continued to kind of whine and cry, I leaned over and asked him, "Are you sick?" Through a bunch of muttering and carrying on, he was telling me that he had been unfaithful to his wife while he was on R&R in Tokyo. He was so sorry that he had done that and that she didn't deserve what he had done. He hoped she wouldn't find out and if she did would she forgive him? This went on for most of my two-hour shift.

When you went on R&R you invariably got a package deal at a hotel. A girl came with it. They hand you this girl that you hadn't expected, or maybe didn't really want, but it just seems like you can't turn the deal down, and there you go. The thing that makes you go along with it all is the hellish seven months that you have just put in. In a lot of cases you are lucky to be alive. And it's not over yet. You have to go back and do it all over again! You feel like you have to. You may not get another chance.

It was cold up on line. I didn't realize how cold or how lucky I was to be on the south side of the hill. I was outside our bunker when Norm Sherman, from our third platoon, came over the hill from his forward position. As we met I could see he was shivering and was a whitish-blue in the face. You just wanted to hug him and warm him up! "That damn wind chills you to the bone!" he said. "We don't get any sun to warm ya up either." He was wearing wool and polyester long johns over his underwear. We all had top and bottom fatigues, a pile jacket, a field jacket, a parka with a fur-lined hood, a pile cap with ear flaps, and a scarf and liners inside our mittens. We wore so-called wind proof pants over our fatigues and had snow-pac boots on our feet that were ten times better than the boots the poor guys wore the first winter over here. Norm and his bunker buddy had sleeping bags and maybe they could seal out the wind a little with their ponchos. It was nasty duty in those forward bunkers! The Chinese were cold too. There wasn't much going on around us, but there was always a fierce battle going on somewhere.

Several months before the army decided to integrate the last of its all-black units into regular units in Korea. So now Fox Company was getting two black soldiers. One of the black guys didn't get a fair shake. Instead of putting him in a bunker with a regular Fox Company soldier, they put him in a bunker with a South Korean ROK soldier who probably couldn't even speak English. I don't know if they did this with the other black guy or not. Anyway, we were rotating down the bunkers and sending a couple of guys each day down the hill to get a shower. It was the black guy's turn to go down and get a shower.

After he had left, his squad leader went over to see how the South Korean soldier was doing and found him face down in the bunker with a bayonet in his back. He was dead! Of course, the company lieutenant was told right away. Our little switchboard was buzzing. The lieutenant was on the line telling battalion of our problem. They couldn't help but suspect that the black soldier had killed the Korean. The MPs were sent over to the shower tent and arrested the black guy. He never returned to Fox Company. Around this time there had been some serious damage caused by infiltrators behind the line. For the previous two weeks, we had been using passwords each night just in case we confronted someone strange. There was a new password each night. After dark, us runners would scoot on out to our platoon CPs and give them the new password. On the night of the murder in the bunker, I picked my way across the steep, rocky cliff on the way to the third platoon. It was kind of scary negotiating those rocks at night. As I got close to the CP bunker, I could hear there was a commotion going on inside. I loudly said, "It's Rasmussen," as I pushed aside the poncho covering the doorway and went on in. In the candlelight I could see this other black soldier lying on his back on the floor of the bunker. He was flailing his arms and legs and half crying and hollering, "I ain't going out in that hole. There's a murderer out there. I can't, I can't." He said this over and over without stop. And he just kept on. I looked at Bob. He was shaking his head. I could see this was no place for me, so I gave the password to the platoon sergeant and got out of there. I never talked to Bob about this or heard anymore about it. I'm sure that that black guy didn't stay in Fox Company either.

You can't pass judgment on soldiers. Like everybody else, they have different tolerances for stress and bad situations. You never know until you go through it. Maybe these two blacks were near their "I can't take it anymore" point from fierce fighting back in their old unit. You don't know. It's easy to become a coward when you are tired and afraid. With good leadership, black soldiers did themselves proud in Korea! I always remembered, when we were being trucked to the front line, the four truckloads of Ethiopian soldiers we slowly passed. They were small guys and they were really black. They were there as part of the United Nations force.

Black people can trace some of their beliefs, superstitions, and fears way back. Ancient rituals practiced by African tribes were brought to this country by the slaves. These rituals and traditions were transformed and blended with other world beliefs, particularly Roman Catholicism. It all evolved into the voodoo religion. It maintained a lot of the old original African beliefs that arrived in strange ways. The old African tribesmen looked to the heavens with fear and for answers. That was how the snake became a vehicle to God and the spirits.

Any snake that is wet with water will reflect a rainbow of colors off its scales when the light is right. This was a reflection of God's rainbows in the heavens. So the snake became a very important part of these rituals and voodoo religion, especially the python. It is actually a God that has a special name! The scorpion and all kinds of things took on importance. Ancient missionaries may have told the tribesmen about Greek astrologers and their "Scorpious" in the sky. This is the constellation that is shaped like a scorpion. So, the scorpion became a part of voodoo. The tribesmen also burned incense and candles and even had shrunken heads around. All of this stuff was positive and good. Voodoo is a positive religion! They believe that there is energy in all things and that they can withdraw this positive energy to do good. That is why they had voodoo dolls and wood statues that represented things like love, health, and happiness. By sticking pins in these dolls and pounding nails into these statues, they could withdraw their power and spirits, which would make things better. The blood from a chicken could do the same.

Africans who believed in voodoo revered their dead. They made sure their souls were taken care of. Their ancestors were still a part of their life. They had rituals to contact the dead or made offerings to the dead. These rituals had special dancing and costumes, spiritual drums with different beats, animal bloodletting, and of course pythons

In this country, black slaves were, for the most part, forbidden to practice voodoo on plantations. When a black on the plantation died, he or she was just thrown in the ground in the corner of a field. There was no ceremony of any kind. This upset the blacks terribly because to them they would be lost souls. These dead ancestors were going to be very angry because they didn't get a spiritual soul-separating sendoff. So blacks came to believe that these angry lost souls would get out of their graves at night and wander around. They wouldn't have all their human features and would walk around as if in a trance and would be dangerous. The living blacks were scared to death of this happening. They didn't want to go out at night for fear they would meet up with one of these "walking dead." They also called them zombies. Hollywood movies capitalized on this misunderstood religion and magnified the negative stuff about voodoo. We were always afraid of the sinister voodoo people in movies and zombies were really frightening. Somewhere along the line, the practice of sticking pins into dolls to put a deadly curse or malady on someone became a belief. Just the opposite of what was true of voodoo. There were times, in old New Orleans, that voodoo practitioners took advantage of these misdirected curses to intimidate certain people or situations.

We visited New Orleans in 1998. Much of the stuff above was told to us at the Old Voodoo Museum, just off Bourbon Street in the French Quarter. When I asked the knowledgeable fellow about zombies, he related that tale. While we were talking to this guy who was dressed like a voodoo practitioner and had braided hair, I reached down and touched a tarot card that was lying on a table with the rest of the deck. This really upset him and he waved his finger at me and scolded me. I got the idea that the cards were very holy and contained all the answers.

They had two pythons at the museum. One was twelve feet long, and the other eleven feet. While we were there, the eleven-footer was out in the courtyard getting some exercise. The man with the snake had the front part of it draped over his shoulder and across his lap. He asked us if we would like to pet it! My animal-loving daughter rushed over and sat beside this caretaker. With the front part and the head hovering over her lap, I took her picture petting this scary reptile. The man said the snake had eaten two rabbits two weeks ago. He said pythons are pretty docile unless they are hungry, provoked, or hurt. In that case, the python was very quick and clever at crushing you to death. That damn snake was six feet from the door when we came back into the courtyard from the back section of the museum. The caretaker was at the other end of the courtyard talking to some guy. The python was slowly poking his snout this way and that.

As far as I was concerned, this forked tongue creature with the vertical eyes was loose and it was time for me to get the hell out of there!

Today, there is a genuine voodoo village in South Carolina. It is in the swamps forty-five miles south of Charleston. It is called Oyotunji. They have a Native American chief who has studied and been ordained for his priesthood on the slave coast of West Africa. Arts and Entertainment Television ran a one-hour special on this priest and this village.

Voodoo is still practiced in New Orleans today. Superstitions seem to be passed on in the South. Ralph Emery tells Halloween ghost stories on Country Music Television out of Nashville. It's been published, that today, forty-five percent of all murders in the United States are committed in five southern states. Some of this stuff sticks with you, if you have been around it!

R&R
(REST AND RECUPERATION)

Up on line, there was one week left in January. I had been told that I had made corporal. That surprised me. I also had been told that I was to head down the hill, early in the morning, and go on R&R to Tokyo. That was kind of unexpected too, and made your mind run things around that had been tucked away for seven months.

It was damn cold as I made my way down the hill to the waiting stake truck. I didn't have my parka on, just my pile jacket and my field jacket. There were only three of us loading up on the truck. One lucky guy got to sit up front with the driver. This other fellow and I were in the back. I don't know what the chill factor was as the truck bucked the wind, but that was one cold ride. We had to go to an airfield south of Seoul where the transport planes were waiting for us. The rumor mill, like always, was busy saying, "One of these planes went down in the sea, killing all on board."

There were about forty-five guys on board our four-engine plane. Maybe a third of us guys were off the line and the rest were support guys. Us guys off the line kind of stunk out, as we hadn't had a change of clothes for a month. We really hadn't even washed our hands and face for a month. It was kind of a neat airplane ride! It was the second time I had ever been in the air.

Our lack of cleanliness was taken care of right at the airport in Tokyo. First, we got a good hot shower and then a new wool olive drab winter uniform with the Eisenhower jacket. We were starving by then, but that was taken care of too! Still at the airport, we went into this nice dining hall. They had a buffet-type serving line. There behind this beautiful food were these God-like creatures with shiny hair and bright eyes and a smile of welcome. They were American women. Volunteers, wives, and mothers that were serving us with all the warmth they could generate toward us guys. It was nice. I guess they knew our last meal might have been a can of beans eaten in a hole somewhere. So, there were seconds and thirds if you wanted them. All the steaks and ice cream you could hold. R&R was starting out just unbelievably!

It was dark by the time we were done eating. The days were short and cool as January is the middle of their winter. We were given an adequate amount of military scrip and told we were on our own, but to be back at 0800 in three days. I had kind of buddied up with a guy from Fox Company and a guy from Easy Company. We had sat near each other on the plane and ate together at that fabulous feast. So we three guys decided to stick together for the next three days. As we left the terminal and looked around in the dimly lit surroundings, we saw a lot of cars parked out there at the curb. Most of them were taxis, but right out front were a half dozen shiny black four-door sedans with a chauffeur standing outside each one. These guys were trying to get our attention and motioning us over. We went right out to one of them and he put out his sales pitch. "Very nice hotel," he said in his broken English, bowing a little

Sam Ingram and Norm Sherman. (L-R) Norm worked for Caterpillar Tractor in Peoria, Ill. Norm was so cold one day I wanted to hug him. See their machine gun barrel.

BATTLEFIELD PROMOTION

Fox Company moved off the line and back into reserve a few days after I returned from R&R. We always had ready access to the Fox Company rotation home list and Leo Wright, our capable likable communication sergeant, was sitting right on top of it. By the end of the first week of February 1952, he was gone, headed home to his farm in Illinois. As I was walking back to our squad tent in reserve area, First Sergeant Collins hollered at me, "Hey Rasmussen, come over here." As I walked up to him, he said, "You got any beer left?" We had been issued our two cans for the week yesterday. "Yeah, I've got my two cans yet," I answered in a puzzled way. "Well, go get 'em," the sergeant said, "I want to talk to you." We opened my two cans of beer in the sergeant's tent. He didn't waste any time in saying, "Now that Leo Wright has gone home, we need a new communications sergeant. How would you like the job?"

This was a huge surprise. I really wasn't sure these upper promotions came right out of the ranks as the guys rotated home. He went on to say, "You'll be rotating home in two or three months and then someone else will have to fill the job." I think that last statement of his helped me with my confidence. So, with a little enthusiasm I accepted the job. Gosh, me being a buck sergeant over four men, who would have thought it? I wonder if Leo Wright had done any recommending? Harold Behling, our second platoon runner, wasn't too happy about it, as he thought he would be getting the job. He was a regular army enlistee and was in the company CP before I was, but I had been in Korea longer than he had. I told him he was in line to get the job when I rotated home, but that didn't help. Things between him and me weren't ever the same.

Bruce Conner, the first platoon runner, would have made a good commo sergeant, but he was fourth on the rotation list and was going home in a couple of weeks too. He went home a corporal. Bruce and I had put on some boxing gloves when we were in a reserve area a couple of times back. I hit him in the nose with a stiff left jab and the blood squirted, making him very mad. He came at me with fists flailing and we got tangled up, fell down, and tumbled down the hill. Laying down there in a heap, we figured that we had had enough. He had caught my nose coming in, bending it a good ninety degrees, but it didn't bleed. We both had very sore noses for a month! Bruce was a fine soldier. It was kind of dumb to box each other though. We didn't have mouthpieces to protect our teeth and there were many other ways to get hurt without injuring each other.

Reserve didn't last very long again. This time we moved up on line way east of Seoul. The hills were higher, it was colder, and there was more snow up there. Our communications bunker was a new one that the troops had been working on. It had a roof, but one side was open to the elements. It was going to be a good one when it was finished. When we hooked up our switchboard we found we had a bad drop module leaving us with only five circuits.

One of the platoons didn't have a phone that night. We got a new drop module sent up from battalion the next day. Harold Behling helped me put it in. Fox Company only stayed in those bunker positions two nights. We didn't have a chance to work on the missing wall of the bunker. Early the third night, for some reason only God knew, the company moved about a mile to our left. Moving in the dark like that could have been a nasty undertaking, but there was a bright half-moon shining on the snow and gave us a lot of light. Some of the canyons we had to cross had waist deep snow in 'em. With that forty-pound switchboard weighing us down, we would sink up to our crotch in the drifts. Harold and I took turns carrying the switchboard. The other three guys had a couple spools of wire and we all had to carry our sleeping bags. We didn't always go up on line with a full complement of radios. It was strange we could find our way to a new position a mile away in the dark.

The five of us found our bunker and it was the pits. It was the smallest bunker we had ever been in. It was more like a cave with very little timber in the roof. We didn't get any communications set up until the next morning. All this commotion and moving on the front line was being done to get units of the United Nations up on line and back into reserve when and if they were ready for these moves. It was a good thing the Chinese didn't know we were so disorganized much of the time.

Out in front of us, the Chinese were up to something. Sergeant Collins called me out of our bunker the second day and told me, "We're sending a couple guys down on a listening post tonight. They'll need a sound powered phone and enough wire to get them down about twenty-five yards. A couple of guys from the platoons will be here at nightfall.

I'll show 'em about where we want them to go. So, have that stuff ready. OK?" I told him I would. This was the first time we had ever sent down a listening post from the company CP. It was a common thing done though. The bad part of being on one of these things is when the enemy gets close enough for you to hear him, it's a dumb time to start whistling and blabbing on the telephone, because then he'll hear where you are too. Nightfall came, the guys showed up, and they were sent down the hill in front of us. We had a sound powered phone in our bunker and they made contact with us after they got hooked up. They were supposed to check in by whistling to us every hour on the hour. Eight and nine o'clock they checked in. At ten o'clock we didn't hear from them.

We thought they had just screwed up. They didn't call at eleven either. We tried calling them. Nothing. I decided to go out and trace the wire for a ways. With the wire between my legs, I was bent over and going hand over hand. It was one of those nights when it's hard to see your hand in front of your face. We were socked in by clouds. If I had taken another step, I would have rammed my helmet into the track of a tank. "Jesus," my brain thought out the word, "that was startling." That big son of a bitch scared me to death. The wire in my hand was caught under the track. Now, sneaking up on a tank in the middle of the night is a good way to get yourself killed. I don't know if they were sitting in their turret on guard or if all the crew was down inside waiting for instructions over their radio? I didn't try to find out. I dropped the wire and quietly sneaked away. They had brought two tanks up on the crest of the hill, so they could fire point blank into the hills across from us. The tank treads had cut our wire into little pieces. I went right on up to the lieutenant and sergeant's bunker. "Sergeant Collins," I said outside. And then again a little louder as I pushed aside the covering on the door, "Sergeant?" "Yeah Rasmussen," he sleepily muttered. I told him about the tanks and our wire. "That's crappy," he said. "We'll just have to leave them guys on the post down there till morning. Thanks for letting me know." I don't think the lieutenant was told about the tanks.

We didn't send down any more listening posts, but they brought them two tanks up into position for three nights in a row. No fighting or problems developed out in front of us during this time. It was still strange how those tanks could come and go without us hearing their rumble and engines. They were only about twenty-five yards from us. They came after dark and left before daybreak. We were always in our cave at those times and it must have been pretty soundproof in there.

It was after the second night that the tanks had been there. Sunrise was taking place outside our bunker. I was awake, laying in my sleeping bag. I had unzipped the bag halfway. All of a sudden, the roof and wall over my legs let go of about 200 pounds of dirt. It was heavy, but it was more scary than anything. I kicked and drew my legs up until they were free and got out of the bag in a hurry and went outside. All of the guys followed me out. We were concerned about this. The damn cave-like bunker was playing games with us. We decided we had to go in and beat on the walls and roof with our gun butts and see if any more dirt was loose. We beat around on the dirt part of the bunker and nothing else came down, so we decided it was a safe place to live. If I had had my sleeping bag zipped up to my neck and that dirt had fallen on my face and upper body, it would have been real panic time. I think the vibrations that the tanks sent through the ground probably caused that dirt to get loose. Fox Company only stayed in this position for about a week and a half. Back to the rear we went.

Russia had proposed peace talks on 23 June 1951. The first useless meeting was on 10 July 1951. Now that we were into February 1952, the peace talks between the United Nations and North Koreans had been going on for about eight months. Deadly fighting, like Heartbreak Ridge, continued on here and there. Then there were the everyday smaller skirmishes all across the line. Both sides were trying to win a bargaining chip. They were just plain playing checkers with human lives.

In reserve area. Leo Wright, our communications sergeant. He was a farmer from Illinois. A number one guy! Working on a "walkie talkie."

Bruce Connor, another number one guy in our company CP. Him and I put on boxing gloves in reserve. Dumb!

MOUNTAINS GOT HIGHER

There was evidence of a big buildup of men and equipment by the Chinese and North Koreans north of Seoul. For centuries the main route of invasion from North Korea to South Korea was the twisting road through the pass north of Seoul. We got the word that they were going to move some marines from the eastern part of the line over to beef up this area north of Seoul. We were to go up and fill the vacant positions left by the marines.

Off and on they would send up an advance party to scout the positions we were going to move into. Being communications sergeant I was going to be going on this advance party. It was during this ride east, in the back of a stake truck, that I saw my first group of South Korean civilians acting out a normal peacetime happening. They were having a funeral. It was a small procession of twenty-five to thirty people on foot. It was kind of like a high school band in a parade. There was oriental music coming out of drums and horns and funny string instruments. There were banners and color. It was interesting. They were taking a person up to the burial hill. There he would be buried standing up. How much money he had and his position in the village would determine how high on the hill he would be buried. Rich leaders were buried toward the top, poor farmers toward the bottom. It was their custom and culture. During those truck rides through the rear, you saw a lot of signs along the road warning you about Korean whiskey. The signs stated, "Korean Whiskey Kills." It must have been made out of gasoline or worse and was available to rear support people. I never saw any myself.

The mountains loomed bigger and bigger as we neared our destination. When we arrived at a staging area, we were met by guys from the companies up on the hill. I was matched up with a guy from the company CP that Fox Company was going to replace. The climb up was certainly longer, but wasn't too bad. The snow had all melted. I met their commo sergeant and went into their bunker. Damn, another small crowded bunker. It was so crowded that I spent the next two nights sleeping sitting up on the floor. There wasn't even room for my pack. He had me store it in a collapsed bunker below theirs. These guys we were replacing were not United States Marines.

The next day, having nothing to do, I followed the well-worn path over to the third platoon CP. Just killing time. I said hello to a couple of guys. Below the third platoon CP was a large, pretty flat area cleared of all trees. They would use the clearing for a chow area whenever warm chow was brought up. I walked across the clearing and had just entered a scattered stand of small birch-like trees when I heard the whining roar of an incoming round. The sound startled me and I jerked around just in time to see the explosion in the clearing.

Suspended in the middle of this explosion of dirt, jagged metal, and burning powder was the body of a soldier. He fell to the ground along with the dirt and other debris.

"Jesus," I thought to myself, "what am I supposed to do now? Is there another round coming in? Am I supposed to hit the dirt?" I just stood there. In a few seconds three guys from the CP rushed down and were trying to administer to him. Immediately one of the guys ran back up to the CP. Another guy with a first aid kit ran down. I just stood where I was, and watched. It couldn't have been much over five minutes when the whop-whop-whop of a helicopter filled the morbid atmosphere. It was a MASH helicopter from nearby. The chopper came in like it had been there before, just clearing the trees from the south, trying to stay below the crest of the hill and out of sight of the Chinese. The medics jumped out of the chopper. I think they already had their hypodermic needles in hand. The soldier was sedated, tourniquets put on bleeding limbs, wrapped in blankets, and placed in one of the two coffins that ride the skid rails. And they were gone. The guys that were trying to help went back up to the CP. I slowly went over to where the round had just hit.

The soldier's bloody helmet was still lying beside the small crater. It had a couple of dents and a single hole the size of a quarter in it. I think the soldier was in real trouble. I went up to the CP where a couple of guys still stood. In talking to them, I found out the Chinese had a Russian mobile 76mm artillery piece out in front of them. It had been harassing them like this for some time. It would fire a single round and then fall quiet. They would move it at night and then fire from a new location. They hadn't been able to find it. If the Chinks had fired that round about two minutes sooner, they might have got me crossing the clearing. It's not funny, but peculiar! That guy was leaving the hill in the morning.

The next day was moving day. The guys on the hill were getting ready to pull out as I headed down the hill to meet up with Fox Company. I pointed out to our group about where we had to go and how we had to snake our way up there. The gears in the head of Fox Company's Jeep driver were rapidly meshing. He was always trying to help. He had a brand new Jeep, just off the assembly line back home. He thought he could drive up that mountain for a long ways, pointing out a clearing here and a clearing there. By driving up with a load of our stuff we would get up there faster and easier. He cleared it with the lieutenant. So, we loaded our switchboard, wire, phones, the lieutenant's and first sergeant's stuff, all our packs, and weapons and ammo into the Jeep. Off the road and up the hill he went, with the Jeep in four-wheel drive.

The five of us followed behind him with no loads on our backs. The lieutenant went the long way. Right away, the Jeep and us were working hard cause it was steep going. The mountain was moist from melted snow, so the tires were constantly taking turns spinning. We pushed it along several times. About one third of the way up, all five of us guys were pushing with all our strength as all four wheels were spinning going nowhere. A big bang and a puff of smoke came out of the Jeep's engine compartment. The engine had seized up! The brand new Jeep wasn't broken in or up to the task. Now, we had to carry all the stuff in the back, straight up to our positions. The Jeep driver made two trips himself, still trying to help. It wasn't a real good idea he had from the beginning.

By late afternoon we had settled into our bunker and had all the phones working. I went down to the collapsed bunker where I had stashed my pack a couple of days ago. It was obvious that someone had been into it. It was out of sight in that bunker and only the five guys from the last crew knew it was down there. Damn those guys. They were headed for reserve and would be restocked. Why did they take my stuff that I needed up here? They took my little camera, my two extra pairs of socks, the flashlight my folks had just sent me, and my two loaded thirty-round magazine clips for my carbine. Those thirty-round clips were hard to come by.

Human beings are complex. They can be so nasty as to drink your last swallow of water, or steal your flashlight, ammo, and socks, while you're asleep, but they'll jump into roaring river rapids to pull you to safety. The good, the bad, and the ugly.

The days went by. It seemed to be quiet around us. I hadn't heard of that Russian artillery piece firing again. It turned cold and snowed an inch. In a couple days it snowed another inch and a half covering everything in a good two inches of the white stuff. The temperature hung just below freezing. Cecil Wood, a good looking kid from Arizona, was pulling his hour of guard in a bunker just over the crest of the hill from the company CP. Cecil was married and had a new little baby girl back home that he had never seen. He had a couple pictures of his new baby and was proud to show them to you. Cecil had good reason to want to get back home. The night was quiet and crisp with snow clouds overhead. There wasn't a lot of light because of the heavy clouds.

Staring out into the white darkness Cecil couldn't believe his eyes as he watched a tree trunk slowly disappear and then come back again. His heart started to pound as his eyes made out a snowy figure of a man slowly and quietly coming up the hill. He was dressed in white from head to toe. It was really hard to make him out against the snowy background. Step by step he was getting closer. He was about twenty yards away. Fighting back his excitement and fear, Cecil braced his carbine on the frozen dirt in front of him. It was already loaded with a thirty-round clip.

Putting that ghost in his sights, as best he could, he squeezed off the first round and didn't stop pulling the trigger until all thirty rounds were gone. After the first few rounds were fired, Cecil sensed that the guy had hit the ground, but he kept on firing at the spot where he should be laying. Then all fell quiet. Cecil's buddy, in the bunker, was wide awake and at his side. They whispered about what was out there. The bunkers, on either side of them, were shocked into full attention from the rifle shots. Were there more of them out there in their invisible suits? Was the guy still alive down there? Were we supposed to go down and see if he was still alive? Was he going to sneak away in the night? No one did anything except stare down the hill with all his might, looking for invisible Chinamen. No one else showed up.

It was a relief to have daybreak come. At good light, Cecil and three other guys went down to where the guy had been when Cecil fired at him. He was still there, dead and half frozen. He had two bags of potato masher hand grenades still around his neck. There were five in each bag for a total of ten grenades. They carefully took the grenades from around his neck and left them there. They carried the guy over the crest of the hill and put him down outside our communications bunker. We heard the story Cecil was telling. We all thought Cecil was a hero. We told him over and over again, "Nice going. Good job."

We looked down at this Chinaman lying on his back in the snow. Quite a lot of red blood had stained his white coveralls in the chest area. It kind of looked like a couple of rounds had hit him in the chest. There was no other indication of being hit. This guy was not real young. He had to be in his middle thirties. He was probably an old Chinese army veteran. Maybe he specialized in sneak operations. They found no other weapons on him. His body, the hand grenades, and the stuff in his pockets would all go back to intelligence. They would see what they could learn from him. As I looked some more at this guy I had this feeling of hatred toward him and I was mad at him at the same time. If he was alive I wouldn't mind torturing him a little myself. I felt he was responsible for all the agony and deaths that were going on around us. That sort of crap begins to wear on you. Forgiveness is a long, long ways away. You want to get even. This is why conflicts go on and on for God only knows how long. And yes, that is a terrible fear inside you that it could go on and on and on.

There happened to be a warrant officer with us at the company CP. He was up from the rear and had spent the night in the lieutenant's bunker. He was standing there with us, looking at the dead Chink, when I said, "I wish I had my camera so I could take his picture." With a look of disgust, the warrant officer blurted out, "Jesus man, what do you want his picture for?" That comfortably rear quartered officer hadn't developed any bitterness toward any of this crap.

All of us thought Cecil was a great guy for being alert like he was. Perhaps he not only saved his own life, but the lives of others. There's a chance that that Chinese sneak specialist knew about where the company CP was and was trying to get past the line and over the hill to lob a couple of grenades into the company commander's bunker, and then maybe into ours. In his white outfit it would be hard to see him as he pulled off this coup and made his escape.

We were only in these positions on line for about three weeks. It was strange. We left this position at night in the dark. It meant our section of the line would be unmanned for the night. There may have been a lateral movement of companies to our position like we had done one time. I didn't know. With small reconnaissance planes, which I never ever saw one, and patrols that were still being made by some companies, they could be pretty sure there wasn't an invasion force out in front of us. Anyway, that's what we did.

The pesky snow was still on the ground. I was the last man to leave the company CP. I should have had one of the guys stay behind with me to help lug that forty-pound switchboard. I thought going down hill with it would be no problem. I stuck my head through the webbed belt that you carried the switchboard with, and hit the trail. I hadn't gone ten yards when my feet went out from under me on the slippery snow. The weight of the switchboard was on the downhill side of me and threw my legs high in the air, making me do a 180 degree cartwheel downhill. When I landed, the switchboard was above me and was acting like an anchor and stopped my slide down the hill. What was really funny was that this was the steep way we tried to come up when we burned up the engine in the Jeep. With the switchboard as my anchor, I slid all the way down that mountain to the road. What a night.

It was the last part of February 1952. It was back to the rear for a week and then back up on line in a new position. They seemed to really be jerking us around. In the rear we picked up our sixth company commander since I had joined Fox Company last July. He was a black first lieutenant. He was tall, handsome, physically fit, and every bit an army officer.

Things went on pretty much like always. There were sounds of artillery being fired off and on, and there was the screaming dive of our planes making an air strike on some days. We had been back up on line about a week when the lieutenant came up to me one morning and said he wanted me to take a ride with him over east about three miles. He went on and said, "We'll walk down the hill and get the company Jeep." Just out of habit, I asked him, "Should I bring a radio along?" "Yeah," he nodded in agreement, "you can bring one along." I told a couple of the runners to turn on another radio in about a half hour and kind of hang around it to see if I could transmit to them with any success. Three miles was the rated maximum distance for these old SCR 300s. As the lieutenant and I were walking down the hill, he told me more about why we were going over east. "Last night," he said, as he watched where he stepped, "the Chinese hit the South Korean army unit that is on our Second Battalion's flank. I guess it's pretty bad. Lots of casualties. We're going over and take a look." I said something like, "Wow." Anyway, it sounded like we were on a pretty somber trip. The Chinese and North Koreans had a damn good intelligence system. Without the use of airplanes and a lot of the best radios, they always knew where everybody was. They knew where the British were on the line. They knew where the Turks were and they knew where the less trained and equipped and poorly led South Koreans were. That's why they hit 'em.

The lieutenant had gotten directions as to how to get there. He was doing the driving. On down the road it wasn't hard to tell when we got to the right place. There was a lot of activity trying to get together an evacuation reinforcement operation. There really didn't seem to be many military people around. Mostly South Korean laborers and their bosses were there and strung on up the hill. It was pushing noontime and all these people were being fed. We unloaded from the Jeep and started up the hill following the string of people who were taking their break. It was steep climbing. Halfway up, the lieutenant and I took a breather. They were just passing out a boiled fish head and a medium sized rice ball to the laborers around us. We sat there and watched them eat. They picked and sucked every bit of meat off that fish head including the eyes and they were very careful not to drop a grain of rice. These people had seen better days.

On the way up, there hadn't been any evidence of the horror we were now beginning to see. We were approaching the crest of the hill from the south side. Scattered around on both sides of us were about a hundred dead, naked, and frozen men that in the black of night had met a very brutal death. It wasn't hard to tell the laborers had been up there and stripped them of all their clothes and shoes. Being naked like that made it worse than real life. A lot of the bodies showed their cause of death. Looking around you could see a throat cut, bowels hanging out, heads bashed in, and flesh torn from bones. It wasn't pretty. There were no weapons of any kind lying around.

The lieutenant and I wondered if there were another hundred or more dead men on the other side of the hill. He said he was going to take a look up north. On his belly, with binoculars in hand, he began to creep up to where he could just see over the hill to the north. I told him I was going to try to call the company CP. I put the unfolded seven-foot antennae into the air and started to screw it into the radio. The lieutenant saw this and got after me, "Get that antennae below the crest of the hill!" He just didn't want to be the cause of an artillery barrage from the Chinks.

I called the CP for several minutes, but never got an answer. The lieutenant spent a short time looking up north with his binoculars, but never looked down for more dead men. There really wasn't any way he could help with anything. We talked a little, with him doing all the talking. "They must have hit the South Koreans on a broader base than just here. These dead people must have been brought here from up and down the line. When they're naked like this, you can't tell if they're North Koreans, South Koreans, or Chinese. They all look alike, especially in the dark! It must have been hell!" There weren't any ROK officers or men around. No one for us to really get some information from, so we headed down, got into our Jeep, and went back to our place on the line. I know the lieutenant talked to battalion and told them what he saw and what he thought.

Yes, you do thank your lucky North Star over and over and over again that so far, you haven't had to go through what those men did. We were close a couple of times, but we were lucky. As I have said before, the North Koreans and Chinese had to do most of their attacking at night because of our air cover and superior artillery coverage. Doing this crap at night makes it doubly terrifying. If you survive it too many times, it could force you to beat the wall with your fists because someone rattled a mess kit, or cause you to shoot yourself in the foot to escape, or make you stab your bunker buddy to get put in jail where it was safe. No one knows.

Cecil Wood from Arizona.
Shooting ghosts one night!

FIRST LEG HOME

One of our runners was number one on the rotation home list. His day came and he was gone. He hadn't been in the company CP but a few weeks. This made me number two on the rotation home list. It was the middle of March 1952. The new runner's name was McCormick. He was another good-looking kid with dark hair and a pleasant attitude. The pleasant attitude sure helps when you're part of a team and sleeping five to a bunker. In about two weeks, another Fox Company guy had rotated home making me number one to go home. Harold Bailing couldn't wait for me to leave. He would be the communications sergeant that he wanted to be. First sergeant Collins had already put in the paperwork for Harold's promotion.

On 8 April, I was told to leave the hill and head back home. I was never to see or hear a navy Corsair or Hellcat make a dive and pull up again. Never to hear again the 105mm and 155mm Howitzers boom their message of death. And I was glad. I was at battalion headquarters for a few days and then I spent a day being trucked to Pusan. Pusan is where this entire Korean thing started for me. We were restricted to base at Pusan while a bunch of guys going home accumulated. We then boarded a small transport ship and left Korea on 16 April. I had been in Korea one week short of ten months. Our ship took us to the good-sized port of Sasabo, Japan. We were then trucked to Camp Mower, which was outside of Sasabo. The word we got at Camp Mower was that it would be about a week before we would board the big troop ship home. Sleeping on an army bunk instead of a dirt shelf in a bunker was pretty nice. Resting up for a couple days was great. Everyone was allowed to go into the town of Sasabo everyday as long as you got a pass. A lot of the guys were doing this and would come back and talk about the good time you could have in town. After three days of resting, I decided to go into town with two other guys that had been in Fox Company support. I casually knew them. We had evening chow on the base and then about six o'clock we boarded the army bus at the base and went into town. Curfew at night was midnight sharp. We were told a couple of times that the last bus from town for the base left at 11:30.

Sasabo was a thriving port town. It was still trying to recover from the ravages of World War II seven years before. There was still a shortage of Japanese men for Japanese women because so many men from their generation had been killed off.

This shortage of men was true in Germany and Russia too, where World War II fighting was so savage. One of the guys I was with had already come to town two times, so he knew the ropes. We leisurely walked up the street, from the bus stop, looking around. There were several young girls across the street from us wearing long skirts and sweaters and with brown and white saddle shoes on their feet. They looked just like any young lady back home in America. We had one destination in mind as we made our way up the street. It was a newer building and it was a nightclub, a lot

SECOND LEG HOME

I can't say that my luck had run out, but I was not in a nice two-bunk stateroom for this voyage home. I had lucked out coming over. I was down in the hold, assigned bunk three in row fifty-six with hundreds of other guys. All one thousand and a half of us were up on deck as the anchor was being raised to get underway. There was a smaller Japanese cargo ship docked right next to the *General Black*. The Japs were loading coal into it through a side opening above the waterline. This must have been coal for the coal-fired steam engine. There was a small platform attached below the opening and two twelve-inch planks ran from the platform down to the dock where the supply of coal was. There were three men, dressed in brief loincloths, running this loading operation. One guy on the dock was loading baskets that were attached to the ends of a pole. The other two guys were walking up the plank with the coal in the baskets balanced across their shoulders.

They would first dump one basket into the hold of the ship, and then the other, and then head down the second plank while the other guy was coming up. The walk was pretty steep and there was a balancing problem with maybe eighty pounds of coal across your shoulders. Anyway, I have never forgotten the size of the calf muscles on these guys. They were bigger than their thigh muscles. Loading many tons of coal this way was tough manual labor. It was a rough way to make a living!

Across the upper part of the sheds at the Sasobo dock was a huge yellow sign with black lettering. It read, "Through This Port Pass The Best Dammed Fighting Men In The World." I took a picture of it. The sign was slowly fading in the distance as the *General Black* headed out to sea with these fighting men aboard.

Sick call the very first day on board was a tremendous long line. It stretched over half way around the ship. It was like half the men on board were in line. Maybe half of them were constipated and the other half had things unknown. There were no wounded or bandaged up guys on the ship. They must have gone home some other way.

It was going to take twelve to thirteen days to get to San Francisco. It was pretty bleak down in the hold, so most of the guys spent all day up on deck. The weather was great, so lying around in the sun wasn't all that bad. No problem with seasickness and the chow was oh so good compared to out of the can rations. The steel deck would get warm from the sun, but it never got any softer! Every bit of steel on that ship had a film on it. I think if you wet your finger and then rubbed it on the deck and then tasted it, it would taste salty. Ocean brine, ocean brine everywhere, and not a drop to drink.

In the center of the ship, which was about a half a deck up, they had several loudspeakers that they played music over. The good old navy fed and entertained us! A lot of the guys laid up there and listened. They had recordings of the two top tunes back home. One was Jo Stafford's, "You Belong To Me." Some of the lyrics went:

"See the pyramids along the Nile,
Watch the sunrise on a tropic isle,
Just remember darling, all the while,
You belong to me."

The other one was Johnny Ray's, "Cry." Some of the lyrics went:

"If your sweetheart,
Sends a letter,
Of goodbye, it's no secret,
You'll feel better,
If you cry!"

Off and on during the day, they would play these two tunes over and over again, along with a few other songs. It was great to lie there in the sun with your eyes closed and visualize the pyramids along the Nile and a tropical island with palm trees. Johnny Ray's song made you think of your family and friends. I thought of Marlene too. You would listen and dream and thank God and have this intense happiness inside. You were going home.

It seemed like most of the guys were quiet and just kind of kept to themselves. There were a couple of loud poker games though, that went on below deck everyday.

When you go off and fight in the Far East, you do kind of leave your heart in San Francisco. Here she came. That beautiful, beautiful Golden Gate Bridge. If you have never walked out onto the Golden Gate Bridge, you should mark it down as an important thing to do. What a magnificent structure leading in and out, and guarding a magnificent town!

LAST LEG HOME

As the tugs pushed us along, we passed a dock in the Frisco harbor that read, "Fort Mason." On up further, we slowed to barely a creep and then finally dropped anchor. It was 7 May 1952. I had been overseas just short of one year. I had gone from combat pay, to overseas pay, to mainland pay. The direction for unloading all of us guys was, "Slowly follow the guy in front of you." We boarded ferryboats right away that took us over to Camp Stoneman. We spent three days there getting out of our salty fatigues, getting a stateside uniform, and getting orders that told you where to go next. These orders changed the direction of my life! I really expected that since I was living in California, was drafted out of the state of California, and did my training in California, I would be sent to a base in California to finish out my eight months of the two years. My orders were sending me to Camp Carson, Colorado. I've always wondered why. The troop train we boarded steamed out of California and I never returned, except to visit my sisters. Sad!

We had Pullman sleepers on our troop train for the three-day trip to Colorado. As we headed east through Barstow and on to Needles, California, we were passing through the Mojave Desert. A hundred miles north of us was another Death Valley! Indian women were trying to sell beaded necklaces to us guys on the platform and through the windows of the train at Needles. I think the train stopped there to take on water for the steam engine. It was a hot, hot, hot part of the country. We then rode on to Flagstaff, Arizona and over to Albuquerque, New Mexico. There we turned north and headed into the Colorado Rocky Mountains. Now, California is beautiful, but in a totally different way than Colorado is. They are both beautiful!

At Camp Carson, which is just outside Colorado Springs, Colorado, we were assigned to a barracks and then run through the supply depot. There we got a couple sets of summer khaki dress uniforms and dress shoes. Dress shoes seemed funny. I hadn't been out of boots for a year. We got a couple sets of fatigues too and new boots. After giving us all this stuff they said, "Go home! Be back here in thirty days." We all threw some of this new stuff into a duffel bag and went in different directions.

I boarded a train again and headed for Grand Island, Nebraska, my old hometown. The folks and I were overjoyed to be together again. About three weeks of mom's home cooking and sleeping in my old bed was really nice.

Mom's fried chicken smothered in fresh parsley and then apple pie was what it was all about. The folks and I drove over to Dannebrog, Nebraska to see all the relatives. Dannebrog is a small town that was settled by Danish immigrants long ago. They named their town Dannebrog because the national banner of Denmark is called Dannebrog. Dannebrog is where I had a mule step on the toe of my shoe and he wouldn't get off. Oh, the pain. He was so heavy! Dannebrog was so small, that going out to the cemetery was one of the big things you always did. All the grandparents and people from one hundred years back were buried there. My cousin's farm was always fun too. On this farm a big goose twisted the skin on my brother's arm. He was about six years old. He got a blood blister to go along with the bawling and running to the house. I think it was another visit that same year, when I was seven, that I just about came off the back of a galloping horse. Evald put me on the back of his horse behind the saddle and told me, "Hang onto me around my waist." Now, Evald was a big man. My short arms barely got to the sides of his middle. Off we went into a gallop. Evald was going up and down in the saddle and it seemed like I was going the opposite direction on the rear end of this creature. My arms, clamped onto this moving two hundred pound man, turned to jelly. I was just about to be thrown off when Evald pulled up and slowed to a walk. It was then that I told him that I wanted off! Today, I'm not too fond of horses or mules.

Evald and Lillian grew some watermelons on their farm in the summertime. In the wintertime, when we went over to their farm, Evald would take my dad, my brother, and I out cottontail rabbit hunting. It made it easier to hunt them if there was a little snow on the ground. We could see the rabbit tracks. The four of us would get into a horse drawn wagon and head out to the stubble fields. When a cottontail decided not to run, my brother and I got to shoot at it with dad's .22-caliber rifle. There was laughter when my brother and I couldn't hit it from twenty feet. We ate lots of cottontail rabbits. We watched my dad hang 'em up by the hind legs on nails and skin 'em, and then take out the guts and throw them to the chickens. Mom would fry them up. They were so good. The big jackrabbits were full of boils, so you weren't supposed to eat them.

I visited some of my old school friends in Grand Island and took in three movies at the Capital and Grand theaters. Mom had to have a picture of me in my uniform. My good friend Bob Woodruff drove me up to the Le Ray Studios. They were upstairs above Greenburger's Men's Store. I smiled and had my combat ribbon on. All the while I was home I found it hard to talk about the close calls in Korea. "Did you kill anybody?" I was asked by a couple of people.

The thirty days went really fast. Back at Camp Carson I was assigned to the supply depot where we had gotten our new clothes when we arrived from Korea. Being a buck sergeant, I got a desk in the office part of the depot. Me and another buck sergeant would look over the paperwork the guys would bring in and see who they were and what they were supposed to get in the warehouse. We would check off a couple places and tear off a copy for them to take and keep the original for our records. It was a nice, easy job. We would get in a shipment of guys once or twice a day and a few stragglers at times. The first sergeant in charge of the depot was a nice guy, but probably drank too much. There was some beer drinking in the back room during the day a lot of the time. A couple of times, on Saturday nights, I babysat the first sergeant's two nice kids while he and his wife went into Colorado Springs and danced the night away.

We didn't work Saturday afternoons or Sundays, so we had some free time. I befriended a guy in our barracks that had a 1937 Ford. He and I got out to see a few things. I shared the cost of gas. We went up to Colorado Springs quite often. We took in the Broadmoor Hotel with its ice skating rink, the Garden Of The Gods Park with its grotesque red sandstone formations, and drove up to Pikes Peak.

Pikes Peak was pretty famous. It was a real snaky drive up to the over 14,000-foot summit. But there was a stunning view from up there. In those days, they had an annual race up the peak called the "Pikes Peak Hill Climb." It was a big event. This friend and I also drove up to Denver one weekend and visited my cousin Elloween. She was born on Halloween, so my aunt and uncle named her Elloween. She and her husband took us out to see the famous outdoor "Red Rock Theater" that seats 10,000 people.

When we walked from the stage area up to the last row high above, my cousin had to stop and rest half way up. My soldier friend and I couldn't believe they could be puffing from that climb. We were still in good mountain climbing shape.

The weeks passed on. I took a six-week typing class. It had about twelve hours of class time. I got up to thirty-five words a minute. The army had some educational soft back books that were available to the men. Most of them were self-teaching books. I think this educational stuff was called the USAFE Program, which stood for the United States Armed Forces Education program.

One morning I was really kind of shocked. We were processing through a new group of guys at the supply depot. Standing in front of me was McCormack, the kid that had just joined the Fox Company CP as a platoon runner. He joined us in the communications bunker about a week before I left the hill. He hadn't been in Korea but a few months. I slowly got up and held my hand out to him. As we were shaking hands I said to him, "What in the world are you doing here?" He put his hand on his lower abdomen and told me, "A sniper got me right through here. It happened about a week after you left. I was out stringing a phone line on the front side. I was lucky he hit me where he did, and that I was close to the squad leader's bunker. They saw me twist around and go down and heard me scream out. The two of them came right out and helped me over to their bunker. Their damn sound power phone wasn't working, so the squad leaders buddy took off for the company CP and got some medics coming out. The bullet went all the way through. The squad leader and I were holding our compression bandages on the hole in front and the hole in back. The medics worked me down the hill and back to MASH, where I was airlifted to Japan. The bullet tore my bowel up so I had some peritonitis. Took me months to heal it up. So, here I am. I'm glad I didn't have to go back to Korea!"

"Man, I'm glad too!" I said to him. "I'm glad you're home!" While we talked, we were holding up the line of guys, so I had to say to him, "Well, I guess I better get to work." I shook his hand again and said, "Good luck, see ya." I took the papers from the guy behind him, but before I sat down I noticed this lieutenant over in the other line. I just stood there and looked at him for a half a minute. He had a cane and had to use it as he limped forward in the line. Now, I really had a flash back. No mistaking. This was the lieutenant that had been up front with us all day on that patrol. I knew his face well. This was the lieutenant that I was laying beside when they threw that 105mm artillery round in on us. This was the lieutenant that scared the shit out of me when he hollered, "Medic! Medic!" then told me, "I've been hit in the leg, my leg!" And I couldn't see where his leg had been hit. When you hit the ground, as stuff comes in, you go down on your belly face down. Maybe his leg was torn up in the back and when we both rolled over you couldn't see it. I don't know! It was kind of traumatic mixed with confusion. When my lieutenant screamed that we were moving out, I had to go!

If a lead scout was needed, that was me since Frank was down. All this had happened to us back in August of last year. Here it was, the end of July, just about a year later. And there was the lieutenant with that leg, still hollering out, "I've been torn up by shrapnel and I need a cane to assist me." I wanted to talk to the lieutenant real bad. I don't know what I would have said and it was still hard to walk up to a lieutenant, salute him, and start talking. And I had this line of guys to process through. He limped closer to the other sergeant's desk and then he was gone too.

The three of us came together that morning, at Camp Carson. We had touched each other's lives far off in the mysterious Orient. It was sad to see them home, both wounded. In a few months I would be released from the army. The lieutenant and McCormack would have some time to go too, unless they both got a medical discharge. We would all go our separate ways and get on with our lives, lives that were turned upside down. The people back home knew what we had done. They saw to it that we got some GI benefits to help.

EPILOGUE

It's ironic that Russia, led by the bully monster Joseph Stalin, had needed the help of most of the world in World War II to keep Germany from conquering them. The other bully monster, Hitler, did have plans for the Russians!

In 1945, the last year of World War II, we made Japan lay down their arms. It was at great sacrifice to us. Joseph Stalin then walked in and took some spoils. He took the Kuril Islands from Japan and got Korea divided into two parts, setting up his puppet dictator, Kim Il Sung, in North Korea. He also wanted a say so in the occupation of Japan, but he didn't get it! Stalin supplied and armed North Korea. Then in 1950, he cajoled and coerced Kim Il Sung into attacking South Korea with the idea of enslaving the whole of Korea under Russian communism. It was ironic that after we had defeated Japan in World War II—a Japan that had been so barbaric in China and other places—we had to go fight for and protect them from communism. Japan didn't have an army anymore.

Toward the end of 1950, we and the other United Nations forces had pushed the North Koreans way back up against China. Mao Tse-tung, the dictator of China, then got a pledge of full support from Stalin and sent hordes of Chinamen into Korea to kill and be killed. Stalin then reneged and didn't give Mao full support. A ceasefire could finally come after the bastard Stalin died on 5 March 1953. It was three years after Russia had instigated the Korean conflict that the ceasefire was signed on 27 July 1953.

God, greedy bully monsters keep the world in turmoil! Today, fifty years after the Korean War started, we Americans still have to have 37,000 troops on the 38th parallel to help control the greed. Today's official Pentagon revised figures of American battlefield deaths for the 3-year war are at 33,651 with 3,262 deaths from other causes. Other United Nations countries suffered casualties also. An article out of the Cox News Service on 25 June 2000, which was the 50th anniversary of the start of the war, stated that it is estimated that a combined 3.8 million Orientals lost their lives in those three years. This 3.8 million includes soldiers from China and North and South Korea, and North and South Korean civilians. What a sad sacrifice they were forced to make. Captured Chinese and North Korean soldiers didn't want to be repatriated back to their country. It's not hard to figure out why!